ISLAM

ISLAM

By HENRI MASSÉ

TRANSLATED FROM THE FRENCH BY
HALIDE EDIB

G · P · PUTNAM'S SONS
New York
1938

PRINTED IN THE UNITED STATES OF AMERICA

Contents

Preface

In recent years three orientalists have each offered to the general reader an exposition of Islam based on the researches of specialists in the subject; but, to some extent, all three have written with the same intention. M. Gaudefroy-Demombynes in "Les Institutions Musulmanes," shows by the very title of his book that he means to restrict himself to a statement of facts.

"Le dogme et la Loi de l'Islam," published in 1910 and translated into French by F. Arin (Paris, 1920), the eminent Hungarian scholar Ignace Goldziher, who died in 1921, gave a dogmatic account of Islam in which the elements of historical development were given only secondary consideration. The same may be said of Père Lammens's "Islam, Croyances et Institutions," published in Beirut in 1926, which followed much the same lines as Goldziher's work, though with modifications on certain points of detail which had by that time become necessary. Now to these three fundamental and indispensable books on the subject the present book is added, not with the intention of replacing them, but to add a sketch of the historical evolution of Islam, rather than another categorical exposition.

At a time when the French are celebrating the centenary of their establishment in Algeria, it is good to remember that France became a great Muslem Power in the course of the 19th century. It is true that British India has about 70 million Muslems and that the

Dutch Malay country nearly fifty millions. Therefore the Arab Muslems, about thirty-eight millions, are inferior in numbers to the Indians and the Malays; but they are the majority of those Muslems which are attached to France. L. Massignon's "L'Annuaire," gives the number of Muslems living in North Africa, French Western Africa, French Equatorial Africa, Madagascar, the coasts of Somali, Indo China, and the French settlements of India, as well as the Maghrebins settled in France, as more than 19 million souls. The Muslems of Syria-Lebanon, who are about two millions, are not included in this total. These figures alone relieve one from the necessity of insisting that it is the duty of the French to acquire a sufficient knowledge of Islam, and an understanding of its urgent problems.

THE AUTHOR.

The Translator's Notes

I. Variations in the translation from the French text were all made after consulting the author.

II. The numbers of verses or chapters quoted from the Koran differ mostly in the translation, for they were mostly wrong in the original. Errors were due partly to the carelessness of A. Colin printers partly because Prof. Massé has used Kasmirinski's translation. The translator has used Maulvi Muhammad Ali's English translation (1920, Lahore) for the division of chapters and verses correspond to the original text of the Koran. However, slight alterations of the text had to be done by the translator as Maulvi Muhammad Ali is a member of Ahmadiya sect (a new sect) and has at times taken liberties with the original to suit the teachings of his sect. Please keep them as they are.

III. Capitalization of the English words is left to Putnam and Sons as the house style in general vary a little in publishers. The translator has no objection to having the wording changed whenever it is deemed necessary to suit the American public.

IV. The spelling of the non-English words is taken from Encyclopedia of Islam (English version). But as the translator could not get an English version she had an Englishman control it in the Br. Museum. Though the translator does not always agree with the transliteration of the Encyclopedia of Islam it may be best to follow it for the sake of uniformity.

V. In quoting French reference books the French spelling has been retained.

TRANSLATOR.

ISLAM

CHAPTER I

The Rise of Islam

ISLAM, a religion accepted by more than 240 million human beings in our time, was preached by Muhammed in the early part of the 7th century A.D. in Arabia. Before giving a summary of this great man's life, it will not be superfluous to give a brief account of the Arabic Peninsula and its population. It will enable us to affirm that Arabia, far from being confined to a splendid isolation, as is often supposed, had been open to external influences for a very long time, and the politico-religious revolution realised by Muhammed was already being prepared for by conditions existing before his time.

ARABIA. Arabia is called "Djazirat-al-Arab" by the Arabs, and means the Arabic Peninsula. The Turks and the Persians name it "Arabistan." It is a plateau with volcanic mountains on the west and south and sloping gently towards the Persian Gulf and the plains of the Euphrates. In area it is about one fourth that of Europe, and may be divided naturally into two parts: Tihama (coastal region), and Nejd (central plateau) which is surrounded by deserts.

Western Arabia comprises two principal regions: Hedjaz and Yemen. Hedjaz, which means "Barrier," is the coastal zone, which, between the Red Sea and the mountains, extends from the Sinai Peninsula to the region situated south of Mecca. Its most northerly part, from Sinai to Tabuk, is poor and arid, and was inhabited in ancient times by the Nabatheans who controlled the commerce of those regions. A route—the importance of which will be seen later—skirts the Red Sea, from the Gulf of Akaba to Medina, crossing the beds of several intermittent torrents. Yathrib, which is now known as Medina stands on a volcanic site between the lava bands (harra), and is consequently situated in the midst of fertile lands which have been cultivated since ancient times, more particularly as date groves. On the north of Medina rises the Mount of Ohod where Muhammed fought one of his early battles. The distance from Medina to Mecca is two days' journey on foot. Towards the south, there is the prosperous ancient city of Taif among the mountains, which has now become the summer resort for the people of Mecca, and where one can find European fruits. On the confines of Hedjaz and Yemen, the country becomes more mountainous. The most fertile region of Hedjaz is Sarat, the eastern part of which is inhabited by the Qahtans, the tribe which is known as the mother of all the Yemen tribes.

Yemen, which means "the country to the right," or the Southern land, is also known as "Happy Arabia." It has been famous at all times for the fertility of its soil, and is rich in the culture of coffee bean. Its numerous ruins bear witness to a brilliant political past, of which its ancient capital Sanaa contains the last vestiges. Yemen was explored, after Niebuhr, and Forskal, by two Frenchmen, Arnaud and Joseph Halévy under heroic conditions, and later by Landberg who described more especially the southern region.

The southern coast of Arabia, called the "Coast of Incense," the culture of which, however, has decreased, is called Hadramaut. It is a country of high mountains, deep valleys, and broad deserts; and its inhabitants willingly expatriate themselves in search of fortune elsewhere. Like Yemen it is also scattered with ruins. On the east is the region of Mahra, well-known for its breed of camels.

As for Oman, situated on the southeast, it is also a country of mountains and is very fertile. It possesses several ports on its coasts, and has been the birth-place of those Arab pilots who have left their mark on the history of navigation. Muskat has supplanted its ancient capital Sohar, which was called by an Arab geographer, "The Gate of China."

Finally, along the Persian Gulf, stretch the lowlands of Bahrein, which are known at present as Lhasa (Al-Hasa). This is the country of pearl-fishers and pirates and the richness of its date-groves is proverbial. Great deserts separate it from Western Arabia: to the South the Dahna, and to the North the Nefud. Dahna the Red, so called because of the colour of its sands, is twice the area of France. In the dry season it is absolutely without water, but after the torrential rains of winter it is as green as a meadow, and the Bedouins[1] come to live there for three or four months with their flocks which feed on the grass and satisfy their thirst on the juicy herbs. Driven away in the hot season, the Bedouins go to the borders of the desert. On the north of Nedjd—that is the central plateau which is crossed by the depression of Ouadi-Romma and where water is occasionally found—the

1 Bedouin (Badaouüin) are the people of the Badiya, meaning desert, in opposition to the people of Hadhar, meaning the city folk.

Nefud [2] desert has much the same character as Dahna, but the red sands which are covered with verdure for a season form vast depressions which are broken by rocky mountains. Farther to the north, the Syrian desert, cut into by expanses of rain water, extends towards the Euphrates, and remains partially arid.

THE ARAB TRIBES. It has been pointed out that these deserts are periodically occupied by nomads —or to be more exact by semi-nomads who migrate with their droves of camels, and flocks of sheep and goats. Lammens says: "Half of the nomads would perish of thirst without the milk of their camels. The horse is a beast of luxury, for it needs water, and is bred only in Nejd and Yemen. As for the donkeys which are used in the coastal regions, the Bedouins look down upon them."

What sort of people are these Bedouins then who have played such an important part in the wars of Islam? Their law was always drawn from their tribal organisation, but it is not certain whether totemism was not also a basis of authority. The nucleus of the tribe is the family which possesses more sons than any other family, and which therefore forces the others to recognise the authority of its chief, called "Sheik," and to group themselves around him. Any man who is expelled from his tribe for some delinquency finds himself in a desperate position unless he manages to get the protection of another tribe. This was the case of Muhammed for a short time. Women have much more freedom than the women of the towns, but they are charged with all the domestic work. The occupation of the men consists of stock breeding, hunting, commercial operations and what is known

[2] Nefud is the plural of Nafd, meaning "dune."

as razzias. The razzia (Ghaswa, Rezzou) which has been practiced from time immemorial, is the custom of descending upon a neighbouring tribe and carrying off its flocks and sometimes even its women and children with the purpose of holding them up to ransom. Bloodshed is avoided as much as possible, as it leads to grave reprisals. This deep-rooted tendency of the Bedouins to loot their neighbours has made them a danger to the territories bordering on the desert, ever since ancient times. Apart from spoils gained from the practice of razzia, one of the principal sources of revenue for the Bedouins was and still is, the right to protect caravans which they accompany and often supply with camels. The town dwellers who cross tribal territory have to pay the tax of fraternity, which is also paid by the people living on the borders of the desert when they are powerless to hold back the Bedouins.

According to Biblical tradition, the Arabs are descended from Abraham, those of the North through Ishmael, and those of the South through Qahtan. The division of the Arab tribes into the northern known as Nizarites or Maadites, and the southern known as Yemenites, arises from this tradition; but this division is not absolute, for the Yemenites particularly, have emigrated when driven away by a temporary drought, or perhaps by a progressive dryness which has brought about a change of climate. The Yemenites were forced to leave their lands because of lack of water, just as the Mayas, for the opposite reason of increasing rains were, according to Huntington, forced to emigrate from Guatemala to Yucatan. Later on it will be seen how an economic motive lay behind these emigrations. In any case it is not impossible to consider these migrations as important factors in the development of that antagonism which eventually grew up between the people of the North and the South. One finds this antagonism existing in the time of Muhammed between the people of Mecca (Nizarites) and of Medina (Yemenites).

The northern tribes were named after a legendary ancestor, Nizar or Maad, and they ultimately branched out into two principal groups—Rabia and Modhar. These two groups, before Islam, emigrated to Iraq, and perpetuated their names in regions of the basin of the Euphrates: Diar Rabia and Diar Modhar. From these came many other tribes and to one of them known as the Kureishi, which still exists in the environs of Mecca, Muhammed belonged.

To the South, tribes descended from the Qahtan (there still exists a tribe of that name) became subdivided into two principal groups: the Himyar and the Kahlan, and from them were descended numerous other tribes among which were those of Lakhm, Kinda and Ghassan. It was the last two that really introduced Arabia into history.

KINGDOMS OF SOUTHERN ARABIA. Beginning in the third millennium before the Christian Era, the Babylonian inscriptions mention a kingdom of Magan, under which name it is possible to surmise that of Maan or Main, a kingdom which is known to have included the whole of southern Arabia. A kingdom called Melukh is also mentioned, which may be taken to be the same as Amalek, the kingdom of the Amalekites.

The Arab documents proper are of much later date. The inscriptions of southern Arabia, the oldest of which belong to 800 years before the Christian Era, fall naturally into two groups according to the dialects in which they are written: the Minaen inscriptions of the Kings of Maan, and the Sabaean inscriptions of the Kings of Saba. The Minaen inscriptions were found by Halévy in Sanaa, and by Glaser in the Qataban region. It appears that the oldest Sabaean inscriptions are contemporary with the latest Minaen inscriptions. In any case, the Arabic annals bear witness to there having been three great periods in the South: the Minaen, the Sabaean, and the Himyarite. It was about the second century before the Christian era that supremacy passed from the Sabaeans to the Himyarites—the Homeritae of the classic authors.

These kingdoms of Arabia, which were the gardens of the world's spices, prospered owing to the fertility of their soil, but also because the commercial route from India to Syria followed the coasts of Arabia by land. When progress in navigation led to the adoption of a sea route to India down the Red Sea and across the Indian Ocean, Arabia ceased to be so important as a commercial route, and it may well be that this economic factor led to the decadence of the system of irrigation which then fertilised the country, and traces of which are still to be found. This probably explains the migrations which we have already mentioned, without having to ascribe them entirely to change of climate.

The Himyarites who were settled on the Red Sea coast, found themselves exposed to the attacks of the Abyssinians. From an uncertain date, possibly 500 B.C., Semitic people had begun to emigrate into Abyssinia; and as a result the Ethiopian kingdom under the Axum Dynasty was founded. It preceded closely the kingdom of the Himyarites which maintained itself down to our days, in spite of violent internal upheavals.

Towards the end of the fifth century (A.D.) Judaism and Christianity both had their adherents in the Himyarite kingdom. The king who professed Judaism persecuted his Christian subjects, and they were obliged to ask for protection from the Axumites, a people converted a century earlier to Christianity. The Axumites seized this opportunity to invade and conquer the lands of their origins. Yemen was governed by Abyssinian viceroys up to the time when a descendant of the Himyarites, after asking in vain for help from the Byzantines, managed by the aid of forces sent by the Sasanid Persian Empire to expel the Abyssinians from Yemen. The Byzantines could not have very well helped the Himyarites against the Christian Axumites. Nevertheless southern Arabia gained nothing but a change of masters: it became a Persian province. Its history had ended.

THE KINGDOMS OF NORTHERN ARABIA. Three of the tribes of southern Arabia, the Lakhm, the Ghassan and the Kinda emigrated north and each created a tardy civilisation of its own under Persian or Byzantine influences. Byzantium and Persia had established garrisons along their desert frontiers for the purpose of protecting themselves from the looters of the desert, and these garrisons were composed of Arab recruits. The rapid rise of the Lakhmid and Ghassanid Dynasties was due to their respective tribes being camped on the outskirts of the Syrian desert, where they served as auxiliaries, one to the Sasanids of Persia and the other to the Byzantine Empire.

Naturally this meant perpetual conflict between the two.

The history of the beginnings of the Lakhmid Kingdom with Hira as its capital (near Kufa, and not far from ancient Babylon) is obscured by legend. An important group in Hira belonged to the "Ibad" that is to the Christians who were among the civilising influences on the Bedouins. In time Hira became an intellectual capital. The first among their historically known kings (whose date is known owing to the discovery of his tomb) died in 324. The alliance of these Bedouins with the Persian Mazdaens did not prevent their embracing Nestorian Christianity. The dynasty maintained itself up to the end of the 6th century, when dissensions arose between the Lakhmid king and his Sasanian suzerain, and as a result the vassal king was replaced by a Persian resident. A few years later the Arabs were to take a brilliant revenge at the battle of Dhu-Qar,[1] near Kufa, which was an event pregnant with great results—as important as those of the battles of Cannae or Poitiers. The Arabs realised for the first time that their powerful neighbours were not invincible. The future artisans of Muslem expansion were to remember this lesson.

The Ghassanids, like their kinsmen and enemies the Lakhmids were converted to Christianity (Monophysite),[2] but unlike their adversaries they had no fixed abode. They occupied Phoenician-Palestine territories and a part of the domain of the ancient

1 Not far from ancient Babylon.

2 Those Christians who recognised only one nature of Jesus Christ. The Armenian Church, the Jacobite Church of Syria and the Coptic church in Egypt are the three independent descendants of the Monophysites.

Nabatheans, but they preferred to camp in the region situated south of Damascus. Under Byzantine influence they attained a civilisation superior to that of the Lakhmids. Their history like that of the Lakhmids is saturated with legend. It is, however, certain, that the Emperor Justinian conferred the titles of Phylarch and of Patrice on one of the Ghassanid chiefs of Syrian tribes, and these titles were considered as the highest possible honour at the time. Both the Ghassanids and Lakhmids reached the apogee of their power at the same time in the sixth century, but the conflict between them became intenser, so that by the end of the same century both sides showed signs of exhaustion. Just as it had been between the Sasanian and the Lakhmid Dynasties, so dissensions arose between the Byzantine Empire and the Ghassanid king. At the time of the Muslem conquest the actual power of the Ghassanid dynasty had come to an end.

The third of the southern tribes which emigrated North was that of Kinda, but they came to a halt in central Arabia and founded a state of their own towards the end of the fifth century. They attacked their Lakhmid neighbours successfully at first, but in 529, the year when the Lakhmid power was at its height, they suffered a severe and decisive defeat. Yet, though short-lived, this state was the most important of the three northern Arab kingdoms. For, the other two were subject to greater powers, while the Kindite kingdom was an independent Arab state. Guidi speaks of it as "the first attempt of the Arabs to gather around a common chief and to be led by him." The idea of a centralised Arab state now lacked only the religious element for it to be able to be realised, and that was supplied a little later by Muhammed himself.

ARAB PAGANISM. What was the religion of the Arabs before the advent of Islam? The inscriptions of the South point to it having been worship of the Moon, which was considered to be a male deity, and whose worship overcame that of the Sun, which was considered to be a female deity. On the other hand, the gods called Aththar, Sin, and Nakruh, remind one of the Babylonian gods, Ichtar, Sin and Makruh; and among the many other deities of the time there was a mother goddess called Lat or Ilat. This goddess is found among the Arabs of the northwest, particularly in Hedjaz, in the company of Wadd, Ozza, Hobal and others which are mentioned in the Koran.[1] In southern Arabia, the country of incense, those pagan gods were honoured by burning incense on their altars. It is possible that the Greeks may have borrowed from Arabs through the intermediary of their incense merchants, their gods Apollo, Hermes and Latone (Leto: Lat), just as they borrowed additional letters for their alphabet.

For the religion of the South, our only source of information is the inscriptions, but for that of the northwest we have, in addition to the inscriptions, the evidence left by a few Muslem authors, though it must be accepted with some caution. Particularly in Hedjaz and Nejd there was a cult of Betyles. The name is derived from the Semitic Bait-el, meaning the House of God. These are mentioned in Genesis.[2] They were raised stones which the Arabs called Nasob, and resemble the Menhirs of the

1 Chap. 71:v. 23; Chap. 53:v. 19-20.

2 Chap. 28:18-19; Leviticus, Chap. 26:1; Numbers, Chap. 33-52.

Druids. This cult appears to have been characteristic of their religion. These Betyles were honoured during seasonal festivals, probably in spring and autumn, when the tribes walked in procession round them, and touched them in order to acquire some of the power believed to be hidden in them.

Two of these stones remained in the sacred enclosure of Mecca: the Black Stone, and the Maqam Ibrahim. Lammens says: "It is foolish to speak of household or domestic gods among the Arabs, for these would have been of a private nature. The Arab before Islam had only a public cult, the rare manifestation of which was enough to exhaust his devotional capacity." These Betyles are often found in pairs such as Isaf-Naila, and Lat-Ozza: a dualism to which Islam was to oppose its irreducible monotheism. The Betyles were fixed or portable, and in the latter case they were carried by the tribe in a pavilion erected on a camel, and which was considered sacred. The Betyles afforded protection on the battlefield, and around them soothsayers and pythonesses (compare those of the Hebrews) would beat drums and chant incantations in loud voices in Sadj.[1] Against this low form of priesthood, as against incantations in Sadj and drum-beaters with disheveled hair, Islam was to react vigorously. Muhammed was to condemn Sadj as demoniacal, (see page 36) and refuse to countenance processions or the Betyle priestcraft, and incidentally curtail women's liberty. Only pilgrimages (see page 156) were to be allowed.

Besides this cult of Betyles, there was also the cult of the dead, especially of ancestors. Of this, deriva-

[1] Sadj is defined by Lammens as: "Bouts-rimée, a form of incantation based on rhythmic cadences and brusque alliterated sounds."

tive customs are still preserved among Bedouins. A Bedouin never passes a sepulchre without adding a stone to the pile of stones already there, or without putting a branch on the branches which are laid upon it. For a Bedouin the greatest evil that can befall him is to die away from his tribe. In the old days a sacrifice ordinarily completed the ritual accompanying the burial of the dead, and it was usually a camel that was sacrificed by having its feet cut and being left on the tomb to die. This custom was also prevalent among the Ghassanids even after their conversion to Christianity—a fact which proves the vitality of some pagan customs. Such survival of pagan custom was particularly noticeable at the time of the Omayyad Caliphs, whose orthodoxy was often questioned.

Did the Bedouins believe in the immortality of the soul? It is evident that religious sentiment was stronger among the Southern tribes than among the Northern; but it was the Northern tribes who believed that death did not separate the soul immediately from the body. According to Lammens, the Bedouins imagined the dead to be "peacefully dozing in their dark abode in a semi-conscious state for a time... while women by their chants and strident cries tried to retain the soul which was in haste to leave the mortal body, and men for their part promised to avenge the wrongs of the dead."

As a matter of fact the perpetual warfare which was waged in pagan Arabia led the Arabs to consider vendetta, which they called "Thar," as a religious obligation. "Thar" held an important position in that modest collection of religious concepts, known as "Din-al-Arab" which constituted the indigent moral code of the Arabs before Islam. Blood vengeance based on a vital principle was not merely an outcome of a desire to satisfy their blind instincts, but was rather due to a sense of piety which compelled them to make reparations for the wrongs of the bereaved family—family being for them the fundamental unit, both social and religious. This obligation, as necessary to their sense of honour as the modern duel was to ours, was replaced, a short time before Islam, by a blood-tax known as "Diya." This ransom or blood-tax appears in an alleviated form in the Koran—reminding one of the ancient Talion of the Semites.

A clan spirit or, rather a family religion, was therefore the foundation of Bedouin conscience. It was the origin of all the tendencies which went to make the "Djahiliya" state. Djahiliya (the pre-Islamic era) signifies a state of roughness, even savagery, in opposition to "Hilm" a word which signifies the state of mind of men who are actuated by reason and moral considerations. Nevertheless the Pagan Bedouin also had his own conception of morality, known as "Morowwa" (virtues). It comprised courage to defend his tribe; magnanimity towards his enemies, except in blood feuds; a large hospitality offering food and wine, the partaker of which became thereby inviolable to his host; and loyalty to the given word, which does not prevent the Bedouins from being bad payers, a fact which we gather from some of their poems. Famine at times drove these "eaters of lizards and grasshoppers" to atrocities. They suppressed their daughters, useless mouths, by burying them alive. But did not China for the same reason, drown its daughters only a century ago, and that in spite of imperial edicts against this custom? We know the

Djahiliya Era best through its poetry. Though the dialects of the South disappeared for good, those of the North created the language of the Koran, which was to play a part in all Islamic culture, similar to that of Latin in Western culture. This Arab language, in the course of its normal development, appeared at first in poems which gave information about Bedouin society. Lammens says: "It was the poets who gave the nomads of the pre-Islamic period the moral maxims and semi-religious proverbs which summarised their religious creed, and provided them with a moral breviary. Muhammed had reason to deprecate the poets, for the Koran was to replace those moralists and theologians. But he did not succeed without some difficulty." As will be seen later, Muhammed did not rely on the desert folk; he wanted the support of the town folk. His preaching of One God as opposed to the polytheism of the nomad, was to take root first in the cities. Renan's formula "the desert leads to Monotheism" does not apply to Arabia.

ALIEN INFLUENCES. In the beginning of the 7th century, paganism still dominated the desert; but Tihama, the region of the city-dwellers, was exposed to outside influences of all kinds. In the North, the Lakhmids and the Ghassanids had been intermediaries of foreign influence. But the Christian and Jewish communities were already settled for a long time in Yemen, particularly in Hedjaz. The principal Christian community was that of Nadjran. The Jews, merchants and above all cultivators of the soil, were prospering in Khaibar and Yathrib, the future Medina; and both were struggling for power in Mecca, that city being important because of its proximity to water—a vital factor in a land of droughts.

To the well of Zemzem in Mecca was attached a sanctuary, the Kaaba, near which the caravans passed, for Mecca was naturally on the caravan routes. It was also rapidly becoming a centre of great pagan Fairs for which both the city-dwellers and the Bedouins assembled, these Fairs taking place during the time of truce when the razzias were suspended. Another great Fair took place in Oqaz. Lammens says: "At the time of the annual market the lonely place became animated; merchants pitched their tents and Bedouins recited their latest poems." Just as at the great games of Ancient Greece, so these Arab fairs had their poetic tournaments; and like that of Mecca, Oqaz was a commercial centre with Taif as its principal town, a town of high altitude which was on the caravan route between the Persian Gulf and Nedjd. Nevertheless, in its economic importance it was not equal to Mecca. The latter had a more advantageous position, being nearer to Syria, and to the sea. Further, by the end of the sixth century, the intensified hostilities between Persia and Byzantium, had exhausted both, and unconsciously prepared for the triumph of Islam. This crisis, by closing the routes to Asia, precipitated the decadence of Palmyra and of Hira. It was then that the Persians, whom the Byzantines could not keep back without difficulty, sought for an outlet in Yemen, where they could get control of the route connecting the Far-East to the Mediterranean. Imitating the politics of Augustus, they tried to develop relations with the tribes along the Red Sea, as the Persians were in possession of the Euphrates route. Later, when the first Muslem conquerors entered Mesopotamia, the situation there proved an unfortunate one for Arabia. But under the Abassid Caliphs, when civil wars had rendered the Euphrates-Syria route impracticable, Arabia was to profit by it.

In the early part of the 7th century, the markets of Western Arabia were points of contact between India, Persia, Babylonia, Ethiopia and Syria Palestine, and were therefore, very prosperous. Caravans transported commodities of the most divers character: skins, precious metals, perfumes and aromatics from Arabia; gold dust and ivory from Africa; tissues, arms, cereals, and olive-oil from Syria; silks from China and negro slaves from Abyssinia. Everyone, even women —among whom was Khadidja, the first wife of Muhammed—put their capital into these commercial enterprises by which Hedjaz enjoyed such prosperity.

One must not hesitate to repeat that the preaching of Muhammed was to be addressed to people who for some time already had renounced their savage isolation, and had submitted to military, commercial and religious influences from outside. These influences must be studied a little if one is to understand the genesis of Islam. Lammens says: "Mecca was the centre of a syndicate of financiers, of merchants and of speculators composed of the Kureishites." Welhausen says: "There is no doubt that in Mecca, commerce played the part of a preparatory school of politics." Muhammed himself began as a merchant, and the traces of commercial terms are seen in the Koran. Besides the Kureishite commerce there was also that of Jews and the Christians. What was then the situation in Hedjaz?

JEWS AND CHRISTIANS. Social cohesion among the Jews appears to have been stronger than among the Christians. The Christians belonged to divergent churches, the rivalry between which lessened their power, this being another factor which was to facilitate the conquest of Islam. There were the Nestorian churches of Persia and Ethiopia, the Armenian church and the Egyptian church, each divided by schisms within, and regarding the others as heretics. The Christians were mostly adventurers, dealers in curiosities, wine-merchants, or hired workers, and they lived on the outskirts of the city, while the residences of the old native families were grouped around the Kaaba. In brief, the divisions and isolation of the Christians were not favourable to their forming a real community.

On the other hand, the Jews gave the impression of an organised force, and were systematically grouped, quite differently from the scattered Christians. There was no divergence of religious hierarchy, and their cult was strictly regulated. In Mecca they also lived in the suburbs, but in Yathrib (Medina) they owned land and capital. When Muhammed left Mecca for Medina the warm welcome he received from the natives of that city had something to do with the antagonism felt against the Jewish plutocracy. One can therefore affirm at this stage that Muhammed's intellectual evolution was influenced by this state of affairs. As long as he lived in Mecca, the Judeo-Christian legends which appear in the Koran remained sketchy; but in Medina, where he came in contact with a powerful Jewish community, these legends multiplied in the Koran. It is at that time that Muhammed made Abraham (the father of Ishmael and the ancestor of the Arabs of the North) the founder of Kaaba and the instigator of the pilgrimage to Mecca. This centralising of religious feeling round the Kaaba at Mecca is a fundamental idea of Islam, and one of its generating principles, for it is this which really gave an autonomy to the new religion with respect to Judaism and to paganism.

Abraham is mentioned several times in the Koran under the title of Hanif.[1] It happened that this title designated before Islam those men who confessed neither Christianity nor Judaism, but who aspired vaguely to a religion with less dogma and rites—that is, to an integral monotheism. In the beginning of his career Muhammed did not distinguish clearly the difference between Judaism and Christianity. He respected both as revealed religions with their sacred books. It was a little later that he frankly rejected both in favour of an essentially monotheistic religion, considering them only imperfect forms of Islam. Monotheism definitely crystallised the ideals of the mysterious Hanifs—hence they can be accepted as the forerunners of Muhammed.

MUHAMMED: HIS CHILDHOOD AND YOUTH. It was in this Mecca so diverse in human elements, so intensely alive that even the fever of commerce and money-lending could not stifle the confused dreams of religious souls, that Muhammed was born between 570 (the traditional date) and 580. What we know of his life is based on the scattered allusions in the Koran and on the "Sira"—the compilation begun by Arab historians towards the end of the 7th century. It would not be wrong to say that the traditional "Sira" has partially transformed Muhammed's personality. Though the Prophet himself declared that he was nothing but a man like any other man, the "Sira" introduced the supernatural into his

[1] Chap. 6:v. 80 and 162.

life in a way which makes it parallel with the lives of Moses and Jesus. In spite of Muhammed's human failings, which he was the first to recognise, he became in the Sira an ideal of perfection. In recent years Orientalists have critically examined the Sira, and the essential facts are briefly as follows:

Muhammed's childhood was not happy. His father died before he was born, and his mother Amina when he was six years old. About three or four years after he lost his grandfather Abd-al-Muttalib, and was adopted by his uncle Abu-Talib. Muhammed's family belonged to the Kureishite tribe, the aristocracy of Mecca. The tribe was divided into ten clans. Next to nothing is known about the origins of this tribe. According to tradition, more or less legendary, Mecca was first occupied by the Djorhom tribe. When the southern tribes emigrated to Mecca, that of Khozea remained on Meccan territory, and a few years later evicted the Djorhomites. It was then that the Kureishites appeared on the scene, half shepherds and half looters, who led a nomadic existence in the environs of Mecca, guiding caravans and hiring their camels. One of their members, Qosay, managed to gather round him the dispersed members of the tribe and established himself solidly in Mecca. He recognised the cult which his predecessors had allowed to degenerate, promulgated a real constitution, and established the seat of the government in an edifice known as Dar-al-Nadwa, that is the House of Assembly, near the Kaaba. The Orientalist Caetani compares the part of Qosay rightly to that of Theseus or Romulus. His authority was derived from the functions which became the privileges of the Kureishites and made their fortune: the guiding and feeding of the pilgrims, the guardianship of the military standard, the command of the military expeditions. His eldest son Abd-ed-Dar let his younger brother Abd-Manaf supplant him. Of the four sons of the last, the eldest Abd-Shems, begot Omayya, the ancestor of the Omayyad Caliphs; and the second son, Hashim, was the great-grandfather of Muhammed.

These are the principal facts which emerge from the masses of traditional legends. Genealogically, Muhammed descends from the founder of the city. But in spite of his illustrious origins, his youth was one of much hardship and the Koran alludes to it in this manner: "Did He not find thee an orphan and give thee shelter . . . and find thee unable to see and show thee the Way? Did He not find thee in want and make thee free from want.[1] . . ." In those days Hashim's line was paralysed because of poverty while that of Omayya dominated Mecca.

Mohammed spent several years conducting caravans, and his reputation for honesty procured for him an engagement in the commercial house of Khadidja, a widow. Travelling thus, leading Khadidja's caravans, he met a Christian monk in Syria. Muslem traditions contain several legends in regard to Mohammed's meeting with monks. (Sergius, Bahira, or Nestor). These legends try to show that the Christians had guessed the prophetic character of Mohammed. In the Koran itself the Jewish influence is incontestibly stronger than the Christian. Nevertheless, without following traditions, one must mention the strange coincidence which Tor Andrae has recently found: several passages of the Koran remind one of the texts of the Syriac Edification; the eschato-

[1] Chap. 93:v. 6-8.

logical verses of the Koran, which are the earliest, resemble strangely certain passages of the homilies of Saint Ephrem, the famous oriental doctor whose vehemence is compared to Jeremiah.[1] On the other hand to the Sabaean influence mentioned in the Koran, one has to add the possibility of a Samaritan influence.[2]

It is quite possible that Muhammed's interviews with some Christian monks had made him aware of the mysteries of the beyond. But this awakening did not give immediate results, because, when he was twenty-five he married Khadidja, who was considered older than himself. Nevertheless the marriage was fruitful in more ways than one. When later Muhammed was disturbed and worried by the early revelations, it was Khadidja who soothed him, and his campaigns were sustained by her funds. One can say that Khadidja's influence on the beginnings of Islam was most important. Further she bore him his only daughter, the delicate and melancholic Fatima, who with her husband Ali, promoted Muhammed's line. Muhammed's family, the Sherif Hasanians, and the Sayid Huseinians descend from Fatima's sons—Hasan and Husain. The greatest proof of Khadidja's ascendance over Mohammed is that he did not take another wife during her lifetime.

MUHAMMED: THE REVELATION AND THE EARLY PREACHINGS. Though domestic happiness had retarded Muhammed's mission, it had not turned him away from his religious preoccupations. We do not know whom he frequented in Mecca in the course of his commercial tours, but according to

1 Encyclopedia of Islam, art. Samaritans.

2 Gaudefroy-Demombynes, Rev. His. Religions, 1927.

tradition he retired periodically to a grotto near Mecca, either from personal inclination or through the influence of hermits. However, after a few years of restlessness he heard a voice which at first he took to be that of a malignant spirit. But the voice became clearer, and Khadidja assured him that the voice was not malignant.

What was the nature of these first revelations? One can get an idea of their nature only through a study of the earliest chapters of the Koran, which are also the most beautiful. Certain verses in the 73rd and the 74th chapters tell us that the revelations came usually at night. In those Muhammed does not, properly speaking, appear as a prophet. He is only chosen by Allah as a trustee of divine instructions, which instructions were given to him through the intermediary of a spirit which Muhammed calls at first the angel Israfil, and later the angel Gabriel.[1] In the later revelations Mohammed becomes a "Mondhir," meaning a warner, and a "Resoul" meaning an apostle.

Another verse leads one to understand that Mohammed took a long time before communicating these revelations to his people.[2] It was only after having received definite orders from above that he decided to preach; and then he preached the existence of One God as opposed to paganism polytheism. Further, to those of his contemporaries who loved the good things of this earth, he predicted a resurrection followed by terrible chastisement.[3] The nature of

1 Chap. 2:v. 97-98.
2 Chap. 10:v. 16.
3 Chap. 102:v. 5-7.

this chastisement was not precise as at times it was to be the end of the world, which with time became less imminent—and at times a catastrophe similar to that which destroyed the legendary people of ancient Arabia or the Hebrews. What then must one do to ensure salvation? According to the Koran those who sought salvation "were not enjoined to do anything except that they should serve Allah, being sincerely obedient to Him, upright in their lives, faithful in prayers and regularly paying the poor-rate." That was the right religion.[1] And again it is said in the Koran "... As for Him who gives away freely and is on guard against evil ... we will facilitate for him the easy end.[2] Eternal felicity is described soberly in contrast to the torments which shall overtake the sinful.

This preaching which had a socialist tendency was to turn not only the rich merchants of Mecca against Muhammed, but also the attendants attached to the Kaaba who made their livelihood by the offerings they received from pilgrims. Muhammed expressed himself in short verses, with an abrupt rhythm marked by recurring sounds which, without being quite the same, were reminiscent of the "Sadj" of the pagan divines. When his contemporaries accused him of having assimilated the style of the pagan poets, the accusation was refuted by several verses in the Koran.[3]

The first to believe in Muhammed's word, after his cousin Ali, the son of Abu-Talib, was Khadidja. Ali's extreme youth diminished the importance of his

[1] Chap. 98:v. 5.
[2] Chap. 92:v. 3-7.
[3] Chap. 69:v. 41.

conversion. Much more useful was the conversion of Abu-Bekr, the notable merchant whose attachment to Muhammed remained unshakable. Another permanent supporter of the prophet was his adopted son Zaid. (Voltaire transformed Zaid into Séide, and the word has remained as such in the French language). Apart from the few members of his family, Muhammed surrounded himself by men who belonged to the dispossessed classes whose faith was in danger of being attacked by the Kureishites. Hence these humble converts were advised by Muhammed to emigrate to Abyssinia; which they did, and where they were permitted by the Negus to settle and wait for better days. The sudden conversion of the energetic Omar was to have a decisive effect on the destiny of Islam, but at the moment it did not prevent the split between the Kureishite party and the members of the new religion. It was a decided misfortune for Muslems when Khadidja and Abu-Talib died at this stage. Mohammed, forsaken by his family, and what is graver, by his tribe, sought for support in Taif, but was expelled from there. It was owing to the intervention of a Kureishite that he was allowed to return to Mecca.

HEGIRA. It was about this time that Muhammed met some merchants from Medina. Though unconsciously, the minds of these men were prepared for a monotheistic creed, and their hostility to the people of Mecca made them favour Muhammed. A year later, between 610 and 620, a few Medinites, the future "Ansar," meaning auxiliaries, met Muhammed in secret and took an oath of allegiance. With this Muhammed became the leader of a politico-religious party. According to tradition, Abas, Muhammed's uncle, played an important part at this meeting. This oath was renewed later and henceforth Muhammed could count on the loyalty of the Medinites. In consequence he decided to send his handful of followers to Medina. He himself was the last to emigrate, and less dramatically than it is generally supposed. One day, or rather one night he went. The date was eventually fixed as July 16, 622, and it became the beginning of the Muslem Era, known as the Hegira. The word means emigration and not *Flight* as it is generally believed. The faithful followers who had preceded Muhammed in this emigration to Medina are called the "Muhadjirs" which means the emigrants. The most difficult part of Muhammed's life was over.

MUHAMMED IN MEDINA. Up to this period Muhammed and his followers had remained on the defensive, but henceforward they were to be on the offensive; and this war between the people of Mecca and of Medina was to be economic as well as religious, a fact which is confirmed by a Koranic verse.[1] "Fight those who . . . until they pay the tax in acknowledgment of superiority and are in a state of subjection."

The first thing to be done in Medina was to unify its heterogeneous elements. These were: the native Arabs of Medina; the "Ansar" (the Medinite auxiliaries of Muhammed); the Muhadjirs (Arab emigrants and partisans of Muhammed from Mecca); the Jews. The Medinites belonged to two tribes who were constantly divided by an age-old rivalry, the Aws and the Khazradj. That Muhammed's political ability was as strong as his religious spirit is shown by a docu-

[1] Chap. 9:v. 29.

ment he drew up which was to settle all the differences. It is a precious document because of its authenticity. It set out the rules for the Muslem community and it declared the Muhadjirs and the Ansars to belong to a single community which also included the Jews and the pagans. Hence there were no longer divided clans or divergent interests in Medina, but a united population ready to defend the city against all outside attacks in the name of Allah and under the command of Muhammed. It is superfluous to point out the supreme importance of this act, which, based on the ancient rites of fraternisation, could unite the Arabs from Mecca, the Medinite Arabs and all Muslems and non-Muslems into a single whole. Lammens says: "Mohammed was perhaps the first among his people who attempted to establish a religious fraternity on ties which were not those of race. Nevertheless he was not able to see the ultimate results of this prolific principle. The idea of Islam as a world religion was only realised with the Caliphate." For the time being Muhammed was able to remove the immediate danger of internal rivalries and so continue his work of religious legislation. On the one hand pagan practices were to be eliminated as much as possible, though Muhammed preserved a few of them, notably the institution of pilgrimage. (See page 156.) On the other hand he had to organise a ritual for his religion. Thus he laid down the rules of prayer, instituted ablutions, the call to prayer, and the practice of fasting. The first mosque was built in Medina a little after Muhammed's arrival.

All this, by consolidating Muhammed's authority soon roused the Jews against him; for they were afraid of losing their financial power. But this Jewish hostility was not an open one, therefore the Koran speaks of them as hypocrites. Muhammed in his earlier attempt to arbitrate between the divergent elements of Medina had tried to win over the Jews. His contact with them brought the Old Testament under his notice. A reflection of his conversations with Jews appears in the revelations he received at this date, the annexing of the Patriarch Abraham to Islam being one of the principal results. But it was precisely those passages taken from the Old Testament to which the Jews took exception. The Jews considered the gift of prophecy as the special privilege of Israel, and were not slow to comment on Muhammed's discrepancies in ironical tones. Further, they tried to rekindle the hostility of the native tribes. All these were grave menaces to Muhammed's authority. He broke away from the Jews, named them enemies, and waited for an opportune moment to strike.[1] The most obvious sign of this break is seen in the change in the orientation for the Muslim prayer. After the Hegira, Muhammed had adopted the Jewish orientation, that is, the Muslems were to pray with their faces turned towards Jerusalem. Sixteen or seventeen months later Muhammed declared Abraham to be the founder of Kaaba, and adopted the orientation towards Mecca. Thus the old Arab tradition gained the upper hand over the passing influence of Judaism. This change of orientation in prayer corresponds with a change in politics to which a passage in the Koran alludes.[2]

Hence, from the second year of Hegira onward, the

[1] Koran; Chap. 5:v. 83-86.
[2] Chap. 2:v. 135.

Kaaba became a vital centre for Islam. This conception, already mentioned as fundamental, enabled Muhammed to give a definite goal to his followers—Mecca. He sent them out to the conquest of their religious capital, as well as for the capture of the commercial supremacy which the Kureishites disputed. Thus the razzias began again, their nature differing little from the razzias of pagan days. There is an allusion in the Koran to the inferior courage of the people of Mecca, who had engaged Abyssinian mercenaries—a better disciplined force than the Bedouins. "... if among you there are a hundred patient ones they shall overcome two hundred, and if there are a thousand they shall overcome two thousand...." [1]

The Meccans were vulnerable only on their caravan routes. Muhammed concentrated his efforts on attacking these and thus paralysing their commerce —just as the Barbary Corsairs did a few centuries later. After several unsuccessful attempts, Muhammed's men located a caravan during the sacred month, and this breach of the traditional truce roused great emotion in Medina. A revelation excused the act of the aggressors: "They ask thee concerning the sacred month—whether men shall fight then. Say: fighting then is a grave matter; but hindering men from Allah's way and denying Him, and hindering men from the sacred mosque and turning out its people therefrom are still graver matters with Allah...." [2] As a matter of fact, various incidents of this struggle enabled Muhammed to legislate by means of partial revelations on such divers matters

[1] Chap. 8:v. 66.
[2] Chap. 2:v. 217.

as the division of the land, the spoils of war, the laws of inheritance, and the terms to be accorded to the defeated. The development of these principles will be seen on page 86.

One need not dwell in detail on those expeditions which were mostly skirmishes; but certain facts, serious because of their results, must be mentioned here.

In the second year of the Hegira and in the middle of the month of Ramadan, Muhammed defeated the Meccan forces at Badr, which was a watering place as well as a market place, situated where the route from Medina joined the main caravan routes. Muhammed was informed that an important caravan was on its way from Mecca to Syria, led by Abu-Sofyan, a notable merchant, and leader of the party hostile to Muslems. Muhammed decided to stop it. The Meccans divining Muhammed's intentions, hastily sent an improvised rescue party. The newly arrived forces disorganised the Meccans and created panic among them. Muhammed, by the aid of Abu-Bekr, had remained in shelter. For the first time in person he divided the spoils between the winners, being instructed to do so by a revelation.[1]

A year later the Meccans prepared for revenge. Besides the humiliation of the defeat which had to be wiped out, there was also the important question of the security of the caravans. The Meccans camped on the Mount of Ohod, and forced the Medinites to come out by ravaging their fields. The Medinites, though in a favourable position at first, were eventually defeated by Khalid the Kureishite. The same man was converted to Islam later, after which he became one of the future artisans of Islamic expansion.

[1] Chap. 8:v. 42.

Muhammed himself was surrounded by the enemy and wounded. Nevertheless the Kureishites halted their march before Medina, and dared not attack the city itself. Hence their victory had no morrow.

Muhammed in order to rouse the spirits of his followers after this defeat, at once led them into another battle. The Koran encouraged the waverers.[1] It was during one of these expeditions that Muhammed's favourite wife Ayesha, the daughter of Abu-Bekr, was left behind and brought to the camp by a young Muslem. The incident gave rise to evil rumours. After several days of hesitation Muhammed cleared his young wife's honour by a revelation.[2] Ali, consulted by Muhammed had stood for her repudiation. It is this which was the cause of Ayesha's hatred of Ali to the end of her life. Another revelation [3] allowed Muhammed to marry Zainab (Zenobia) the divorced wife of his faithful Zaid.

In the fifth year of the Hegira a new danger threatened the Muslems. After his break with the Jews, Muhammed had expelled them gradually from Medina, and they had taken refuge at Khaibar where they had persuaded their co-religionists to form a coalition with Meccans and other tribes, hostile to Muhammed. Abu-Sofyan commanded this formidable army, which consisted of excellent troops, the Abyssinian mercenaries. The Muslems could not think of challenging them to open battle. It was then that fortifications appeared in Islam for the first time. A circular ditch was dug all around Medina; the idea is attributed to Selman, a Persian convert.

1 Chap. 3:v. 138.
2 Chap. 24:v. 11.
3 Chap. 33:v. 37.

The allies, surprised, laid siege to the city. After three weeks, a lack of provisions, disunion among the besiegers, as well as Muhammed's diplomatic ability, obliged them to raise the siege. Muhammed had definitely won the day. He had been right in avoiding open battle with Meccan troups, as he was right in harassing the Meccan army with razzias.

In the sixth year of the Hegira he made a grave decision; he went to Mecca during the sacred month. But he stopped at Hudaibiya, a place not far from the city. Delegates from both sides met there in conference and entered upon an agreement by which in the sacred month of the coming year the Kureishites consented to leave Mecca for three days, during which time Muhammed and his faithful followers could enter it. Though it looked as if Muhammed had given way to the demands of his adversaries, in reality it was a great diplomatic success, as he had treated with them as equals. But his followers were disillusioned by being obliged to return to Medina without visiting Kaaba.

Having ensured peace with the Kureishites, the Prophet decided to deal with the Jews. He had reduced those of Medina by taking advantage of the dissensions between the Jewish tribes. But the fortified position of Khaibar was a menace to Medina. It took him and his forces a whole month to reduce the Khaibar forts. This vigorous resistance eventually led to a drastic punishment of the resisters. The Jews lost their property and their lands, and became hired labourers on the lands of their conquerors; and they remained as such until they were finally expelled from Arabia in the time of Caliph Omar. Tradition tells us of an attempt made by a Jew to poison Muhammed, from the effects of which he is said to have suffered for many years; but his symptoms may as easily have been due to malaria so prevalent both in Khaibar and in Medina.

The Treaty of Hudaibiya had put an end to the Muslem attacks on the caravans of Mecca. Therefore Muslems were now seeking their fortunes in Syria. An actual expedition was organised against Transjordanian Arab tribes, then subject to the Byzantine Empire. Did Muhammed undertake this expedition willingly? Was he going to try to extend the natural boundaries of Arabia? However neither he himself nor any of his companions took part in this disastrous expedition. At Muta, near the Dead Sea, Zaid was defeated and killed in battle. Khalid led back to Medina the remains of the defeated army.

This defeat taking place in a far-off land, did not diminish Muhammed's prestige. He was in negotiation with Abu-Sofyan who is described by Lammens as "an accomplished model of liberalism, and of a political system which was adopted later by the Omayyad dynasty." Muhammed had married Abu-Sofyan's daughter, probably a political union such as was contracted by Muhammed with Hafsa, the daughter of Omar, or with Ayesha, the daughter of Abu-Bekr. Abu-Sofyan came to Medina to renew the Treaty of Hudaibiya, but he also promised his son-in-law to prepare the surrender of Mecca. As it was, since the war of Handak (Ditch), Abu-Sofyan had remained neutral, and the marriage of his daughter had finally tied his hands. Muhammed, taking advantage of a quarrel between the tribes in Mecca, marched on it and entered the city without striking a single blow in 630. He had promised an amnesty, and probably also undertook not to remain there. He took possession of Mecca, and returned to Medina after a fortnight's stay.

The surrender of Mecca did not prevent the Bedouins from forming a formidable coalition against Muhammed soon afterwards. This led the Medinites and Meccans to unite against a common enemy for the first time. A surprise attack at night caused panic in their ranks, and without the intervention of Abas, who had so often helped Muhammed, the day might have been fatal for the Muslems. The defeat and surrender of the Bedouins led the inhabitants of Taif, as well as other tribes, to offer their submission. But this submission was only political, and did not necessitate a religious adhesion. We shall see the significance of this after Muhammed's death. The Koran alludes to it in Chapter 49:v.14. "The dwellers of the desert say: we believe. Say: you do not believe; but say: we submit." Muhammed had also to intervene between the Meccans and his Medinite auxiliaries—it was the beginning of a lasting feud between the two.

In 631 Muhammed led a strong army towards Syria, possibly for the purpose of avenging the dead of Muta. But he did not proceed beyond Tabuk, the Byzantine frontiers, contenting himself with several razzias on the borders of the Red Sea. This year, the ninth of the Hegira, is called the "Year of Embassies" by the historians, because of the embassies sent by different tribes to offer submission. Muhammed's power was becoming stronger every day.

On the ninth year of the Hegira, that is in 632, Mohammed made his first and only real pilgrimage to Mecca. He had so far contented himself with the partial pilgrimage called "Omra." The partial pilgrimage takes place outside the appointed time, while "Hadj" which means the real pilgrimage takes place during the time prescribed. (See page 156.) This may have been because he could not lead a party of Muslem pilgrims in person without excluding the pagans; and the pagans were not yet excluded. This exclusion was made in 632 on the authority of a revelation.[1] The same revelation also assured the faithful of economic benefits from this exclusion.

This pilgrimage is known as "the farewell pilgrimage." Muhammed was very tired and ill after his return from Mecca. His indisposition increased, and three months after his return to Medina, he died of pleurisy[2] in June 8, 632.

It is not possible to judge a man like Muhammed in a few lines. In studying his career one perceives at first a man of nervous and restless temperament, a soul mysteriously tormented. His conception of the existence of One God and the reality of the future life became more and more precise. This creed, enforced by a sincere piety, a marvellous gift of eloquence, and a tenacity of purpose, imposed itself on those around him. To these gifts of a prophet, the talents of a statesman, a warrior and a diplomat were added. Muhammed was not a revolutionary, but rather to the contrary. Lammens says: "He preferred to compromise, to transform, to adapt, and finally incorporate." He knew how to wait for the favourable occasion and seize it. He could say, "Time and I." It is true that at his death Islam had not con-

[1] Chap. 9:v. 28.

[2] According to the description of this illness given by Muslem tradition, it looks more like typhoid.

quered Arabia; but it had established itself firmly in Hedjaz. Thanks to Muhammed's religious and political genius, a specially unifying genius of a high order, the Arabs became conscious of their nationhood, and were enabled to emerge from the ignorant and anarchic period of their history, and prepare for their definite entry into the history of civilisation.

CHAPTER II

Arab Hegemony

THE FIRST FOUR CALIPHS. Muhammed, having lost his sons when they were young, left no male offspring. Fatima, the wife of Ali, the only one among his daughters to provide him with male heirs had two sons–Hasan and Husain. A violent political crisis took place immediately after his death. Several conflicting parties were formed, and Medina and Mecca entered upon a struggle for supremacy. Omar dominated the situation, and restored order by recognising Abu-Bekr as Muhammed's successor. This brought Abu-Bekr the vote of the majority, and prevented an early division in Islam. Ali, Muhammed's son-in-law and first convert, could have used his titles to the succession to advantage, but his indecision, a characteristic of his which was to be finally the cause of his downfall, prevented him from organising his partisans. Further, Abu-Bekr's own titles to succession were not negligible. He had been the faithful companion of the Prophet and had remained with him when other Muslems had been obliged to migrate into Abyssinia at a critical time; he had accompanied Muhammed on his migration to Medina to which the Koran alludes: "... there was but one man with him." [1] Moreover his daughter Ayesha had married Muhammed, and though of a pacific tem-

[1] Chapter 9:v. 40.

perament himself, he had stood by Muhammed during his military campaigns. On more pacific occasions Muhammed had entrusted him with important missions, including that of leading the first Muslem pilgrimage to Mecca in the 9th year of the Hegira (631); and finally, Muhammed asked him to preside over the public prayers when he was on his death-bed. This last privilege was the strongest argument in favour of Abu-Bekr's election as Caliph. One also wonders whether Omar, by designating him was not contemplating the exercise of real power behind the nominal authority of a docile old man.

Abu-Bekr's caliphate was in reality the rule of a triumvirate, consisting of himself, Omar, and Abu-Obaida; the last being also a companion of the Prophet and a proven soldier. It was a critical time; the newborn Empire, founded solely on Muhammed's personal authority, threatened to disintegrate; among the Bedouins, some denied Islam openly, others refused to pay taxes he had instituted, or adopted an equivocal attitude. The task before the triumvirate was two-fold. Externally, the razzias were to be carried on as before on the Syrian frontiers, not only for the purpose of preparing for the conquest of that country, but also for the Islamisation of those Arab tribes who had been living on Byzantine territory before Muhammed's time, and who were henceforward to act as agents of penetration. Internally, the continually vacillating tribes called for diplomatic handling, while the apostates and brigands, as well as the definitely hostile tribes demanded a special police control. Besides, as is usually the case, the death of an inspired great leader was followed by a succession of false prophets (there was even a prophetess) who arose in different parts of Arabia. One of them led a fierce resistance in Yamama; the difficult conquest of which incidentally opened up the way to the Bahrein, then under Persian rule. The occupation of Bahrein meant direct contact between the Persians and the Arabs in the Euphrates region. Southern Arabia (Hadramaut) was already pacified by the Arabs.

Hence, during the two years of the reign of Abu-Bekr (632-634) Islam managed to get a firm foothold in Arabia, and began the conquest of parts of Syria and Persia.

Abu-Bekr was succeeded by Omar, whom he had designated as his successor during his lifetime, in accordance with Muslem expectations. Omar reigned for ten years which were a period of triumphant expansion for Islam, during which an enduring administration was achieved. At Omar's death (644), the whole of Persia, Syria and Egypt, as well as Cyrenaica had been conquered by the Muslems and were being regularly administered. If Muhammed was the inspired legislator and the promoter of national unity, then Omar proved the artisan of Islamic expansion. Omar was as simple and austere as the Prophet, or as Abu-Bekr; and remained so even after his brilliant conquests. He reminds one of certain of the soldier-emperors of Ancient Rome. He united in his person all the attributes necessary to a conqueror and an administrator. He was not merely a man of great energy, but one who could make good use of circumstances, people and religious enthusiasm. Lammens says: "His principal and most incontestable merit was to prevent the separatists from taking the upper hand. It was he who laid the foundations of a régime which became increasingly stable under the succeeding Omayyads. Further, it was he who established the principles upon which the conquered states were to be governed, and inaugurated the process of adaptation. It was also during his reign that, by Ali's recommendation, official correspondence began to be dated according to the Hegira, about the 17th or the 18th year of that era.

The conquest of Syria became easier when the Byzantine Empire—exhausted by its wars with the Persians—refused credit hitherto granted to their governors of the frontiers, which had enabled them to recruit mercenaries. After two years of indecisive battles (634-636) the Byzantine forces were decisively defeated by the Arabs at the Battle of Yarmuk. By this defeat the Byzantine Empire lost Syria permanently; and though several villages prolonged a useless resistance for some time, the last capitulated in the year 640.

Their victory at Yarmuk enabled the Arabs to invade the ancient Lakhmid kingdom on Persian territory, and can therefore be considered as the starting point of the Arab invasion of Persia. The success of the Arabs was as usual facilitated by a lack of unity among their adversaries. The old Sasanian Dynasty had wearied the country by its political and religious intolerance; years of war against the Byzantines had drained its resources, and its domains were being continually attacked by the Caucasian Khazars and the Baktrian Turks. The victory of the Arabs at the battle of Kadesya in 637 gave them the possession of Assyria and Chaldea—the Semitic provinces of the Persian Empire. But the Arabs did not stop there: they went on to invade Persia itself, and gained a second victory at Nehawand in 642. This proved decisive, and the complete subjection of Persia became merely a matter of time. Though Persia was now ruled by Arab governors, she did not lose her nationality. Her national sense remains alive throughout the subsequent course of history, but she has to wait for four more centuries for her political renaissance. It is only then that local dynasties are to arise and replace the effete Arab rulers, and themselves become in turn the defenders of the Caliph's Empire against Turkish invasions.[1] This struggle between the Persians and the Turks, which covers centuries, is known as the Wars of Iran and Turan.

In the same year as the battle of Nehawand, the Arabs, after taking Mosul continued their march as far as the capital of Armenia, and sacked it.

Omar had conferred the governorship of Syria on Moawiya, the son of the influential Abu-Sofyan.[2] The nomination proved to be of good service to Moawiya, for eventually he became the founder of the Omayyad Dynasty. It was at the time of his governorship that he proposed to organise a fleet which could easily have been assembled from among the shipping of the coast towns of Syria; but Omar rejected it as an innovation. However Moawiya did form a fleet under Omar's successor; and these armed vessels pestered the Byzantines for years in the Aegean Sea.

The appointment of Moawiya is considered as the indirect cause of the conquest of Egypt. The commander-in-chief of the Syrian army, Amr, of-

[1] See page 76.
[2] See page 59.

fended at being supplanted by Moawiya, led his forces against Egypt, in spite of Omar's opposition, in 640. But as a matter of fact, the Arabs were quick enough to profit by the state of anarchy which reigned in Egypt. That country was torn with religious conflicts, and ravaged by the misrule of the Byzantine governors, just as Persia had been under that of the Sasanians. Amr, after occupying Peluse, waited for reinforcements and won the battle of Heliopolis the moment they arrived. This opened up to the Arabs the way to the suburbs and to the citadel of Babalyum (Cairo). The Nile valley fell into Arab hands. Alexandria surrendered, though not before putting up a stiff resistance, in 642. Four years later the Byzantines recaptured it by a surprise attack; but they were again driven out by the Arabs. The burning of the Alexandrian Library by Omar's orders is pure legend. Egypt was now definitely conquered by the Arabs, and in the meantime Amr had occupied Cyrenaica.

Omar was assassinated by a Persian Christian, but lived long enough to nominate six candidates for the Caliphate. Ali, Muhammed's son-in-law, was one of them; but he was set aside because of his uncompromising attitude: he wanted to reintroduce the early simplicity of Islam under Muhammed, without taking into account the change of conditions which had taken place since. The choice fell on the other son-in-law of Muhammed, Othman the Omayyad, an aged man without energy, and the least capable of continuing Omar's work.

Meanwhile the impetus of Omar's achievements was such that conquests continued systematically: razzias in Asia Minor and the Aegean Islands; military operations in Persia, and raids on North Africa.

Nevertheless, the more distant of these became increasingly difficult; spoils were less abundant; and the conquered peoples embraced Islam not from conviction but in order to pay the lesser tax. On the other hand, Arabs were acquiring a taste for luxury from the conquered, and for the easier life of the subject peoples. This naturally led to financial trouble for which Othman could find no remedy, being mainly occupied endowing the members of his family with appanages. Disorders broke out in the provinces, and the political crisis was rendered acuter by religious unrest. Othman's attempt to issue a definitive text of the Koran increased the hostility he had already inspired among the more rigid believers.[1] One of the most respected companions of Muhammed began to preach, primarily against a general perversion of morals, but also against Othman and the Omayyad family, revindicating at the same time the rights of Ali and his family to the Caliphate. A Jewish convert from Yemen was also propagating Ali's rights to the Caliphate, in Egypt. This reactionary pietist movement was further complicated by political plots, and by the intrigues of Ayesha, Muhammed's young widow, an ambitious woman who was filled with a desire to play a part. All these machinations involved military operations. Othman called together his Syrian forces, on whose loyalty to the Omayyads he could depend. The situation was somewhat like that between Louis XVI and the Army of Princes. Accused of treason, Othman was killed in his house in 656. The question of the legitimacy of Ali's dynasty, and the civil war in Islam date from the end of Othman's reign.

[1] See page 99.

Ali was elected Caliph but not unanimously. Egypt supported him, but it took several days of negotiation to persuade the people of the Sacred Cities and of Iraq to vote for him instead of for his two competitors, Talha and Zubair; the latter being the nephew of Khadidja, Muhammed's first wife. Graver still was the refusal of support from Moawiya, Othman's cousin, the governor of Syria. The result was a lasting and formidable conflict between the older and the younger issues of the Kureishites.

The situation demanded prompt action, but Ali lost everything by his irresolution and his desire for reconciliation. The first days of December, 656, five months after his election to the Caliphate, he left Medina, to which he was never to return, and marched on Basra at the head of his army. It had become essential to defeat Talha and Zubair, the two pretenders to the Caliphate who had taken sides with Ayesha, on the pretext of avenging Othman's death. Actually Ayesha's motive was her lasting hatred of Ali, because of his advice to Muhammed to divorce her years before.[1] Furthermore, she was Zubair's sister-in-law. Ali defeated both his competitors after a hard battle, and Ayesha was taken prisoner and sent to Medina. This first open battle among Muslems themselves is known as the battle of the Camel, because of Ayesha's camel, upon which she rode in an armoured litter. Lammens says: "We find here again the sacred camel and the Qobba (Palladium), but Ayesha, the mother of Muslems, has taken the place of the Betyle . . . the custom is still preserved in the contemporary wars of the Bedouins in the desert. On the sacred camel sits a young girl,

[1] See page 43.

belonging to the noblest family of the tribe, and it is an irreparable dishonour for the tribe to let her fall into enemy hands."

Ali, the victor, was now master of the empire, but it was an empire divided in two by Syria, the stronghold of the Omayyads. Ali's troops occupied Kufa and Ctesiphon, the ancient capital of the Sasanians, then, after crossing the Euphrates at Rakka, his forces met those of Moawiya on the plains of Siffin. It was on this occasion that Moawiya erected a tabernacle, a grand Qobba covered with draperies, in front of which the Syrians took a solemn oath to fight until death. Lammens sees in this the survival of the Palladium [1] which is revealing to a degree of the vitality of pagan customs, particularly under the Omayyads. After three months of uncertain skirmishes, continually interrupted by Ali's negotiations, a decisive battle took place. At a moment when the chances favoured Ali, Amr, the Conqueror of Egypt, saved Moawiya by his strategy. He ordered the Syrian soldiers to tie pages from the Koran on their lances, which meant that they called upon Divine judgment. Ali's companions then forced him to accept arbitration: that meant his ruin. The partisans of vigorous action abandoned him and became his enemies with the same fanaticism as they had been his followers. They withdrew from his camp to the confines of Persia and Mesopotamia, while Ali's representative, a respectable but feeble old man, whose services had been forced upon him, conducted negotiations with Moawiya's delegate, by whom he was hopelessly duped. Those who had abandoned Ali chose a new Caliph for themselves. History gives

[1] See page 24.

them the name of Kharidjites, meaning to come out, to revolt. Those who remained loyal to Ali are known as Shi'ites (from the Arabic word Shi'a meaning partisan). We shall see later, in the fifth chapter, the respective places occupied by these two in Islam.

Ali's position was now tragic, for he was between two fires. On one side Moawiya was proclaimed Caliph by the Syrians as a result of the comedy of arbitration which led to the deposition of Ali; on the other side, the Caliph chosen by the Kharidjites (he is known as anti-Caliph) led his troops into committing all manner of excesses in the Ctesiphon region. Ali marched against the Kharidjites and exterminated them in battle, but quite a number of them had already dispersed into Iraq and Persia where their doctrine gained adherents rapidly before they reached North Africa. Defections from Ali's side began to multiply after this. The people of Kufa retired, and Egypt passed over to Moawiya. After two years of continual fighting against Omayyad invasions in Arabia and Mesopotamia, Ali was assassinated by a Kharidjite in 661.

The place of Ali in history will always be discussed. There are those who consider him as a legendary hero, others take him to have been a very ordinary man. That he was a mediocre politician like the other members of his family, there is no doubt. Pacifism ruined him just as it has done a number of others. He allowed himself to be swept aside through his obstinacy and his blunders. But his sufferings, the tragedy which destroyed his offspring, his character as knight "sans peur et sans reproche," and his idealism as recorded in Islamic traditions, contributed to crown him with the halo of a martyr. It is not surprising that the Shi'ite Muslems should consider him as a saint, while mystics adore him and certain heretics have even raised him to the status of a divinity.

One important result of the foregoing events was that the branch of Abd-Shems, previously eclipsed by the branch of Hashim, came into power, and this meant the triumph of the aristocracy of Mecca. At the same time the Syrian party definitely abolished the electoral system of the Caliphate, made it hereditary, and delegated it permanently to the Omayyad family.

The evolution of the Caliphate under the first four Orthodox Caliphs, known as Rashidun, was in the following stages: stabilisation of Arabia and the preparation for conquest under Abu-Bekr; triumphant expansion under Omar; consolidation of conquests, and weakening of the authority of the Caliphate through ease and luxury under Othman; civil wars, divisions and decadence under Ali; and finally in imitation of the Byzantine and Persian régimes, the founding of a dynasty in place of an elected Caliphate in Islam.

OMAYYAD DYNASTY. When Ali died his faithful followers elected his son Hasan as Caliph. Hasan was an incapable youth, suffering from tuberculosis, and Moawiya induced him to renounce his claims to the Caliphate by paying him liberally. He retired to Medina and died young.

Moawiya's first act of importance was to transfer his capital from Medina to Damascus, where he had for a long time had contact with Byzantine administrative methods. By this change, Moawiya dealt a decisive blow at Ali's partisans who held Medina;

and, after restoring the moral unity of Islam, he reigned for fifteen years as the incontestable master of the Arab world. He realised his projected schemes for a navy, even dared to attack Byzantium. His tolerance towards Christians won for him the lasting loyalty of Syria. He designated his son Yazid as his successor in 680, before he died. The elective system of the Caliphate was at an end.

Yazid's accession did not take place without bloodshed. Hasan's younger brother Husain, who in Moawiya's time had led a retired life, no longer refused to listen to the partisans of his family. He left Medina and joined them at Kufa, but was followed by Omayyad cavalry, and he and his handful of followers were surrounded at Kerbela. For ten days Husain and his escorts waited for developments. The leader of Omayyad troops wanted his surrender without fighting, merely by closing the passage of the Euphrates. At the end of ten days Husain was requested to submit, but he refused. It was a simple matter for the four thousand of Omayyad men to reduce Husain's forces. In the battle Husain's followers were all killed, and he himself fell, pierced in several parts of the body. This event which was unimportant in itself had incalculable political and religious consequences: Shi'ism now had its first martyrs.[1]

After Husain's death the Caliph Yazid had to fight a much more formidable pretender to the Caliphate. This was Abd-Allah, the son of Zubair, and the cousin of Muhammed. He had already disputed the Caliphate to Ali himself at an earlier date; and immediately after Husain's death he proclaimed himself

[1] See page 187.

Caliph in Mecca, and was soon recognised as such throughout all Hedjaz. Yazid's forces defied the Medinites—Abd-Allah's partisans—and ventured an attack on Mecca. Mecca was besieged for two months, during which the Kaaba was burnt when the news of Yazid's death arrived. Abd-Allah was recognised simultaneously in Southern Arabia, Iraq and in parts of Syria. But the rest of the Muslem world remained loyal to the Omayyad Dynasty, in spite of the mediocrity of the next two successors of Yazid. Yazid's third successor, Abd-al-Malik, inherited a much more complex state of affairs. Three pretenders disputed his claims to the Caliphate. They were: Muhammed, the son of Hanifite, the candidate of the Ali'ites; Nadjda, the candidate of the Kharidjites; and Abd-Allah, the son of Zubair. But Abd-al-Malik managed to restore the authority of the Omayyads. Iraq was conquered, Abd-Allah's brother was killed in battle, and Abd-Allah himself perished during the conquest of Mecca by the Omayyads in 692. This was the last attempt made by the older party against the Omayyads. As a matter of fact, under Abd-al-Malik and his successor order reigned throughout the Empire, and wars against Byzantium were resumed, all this being due to the energy of a minister of great ability called Hadjdjadj. Nevertheless, though he was a warrior and an administrator of the first order, the tyranny of Hadjdjadj eventually turned public opinion against the Omayyad Dynasty.

Caliphs succeeded each other rapidly during the first half of the 8th century. But if one omits the long reign of Hasham, who was a conqueror but an indifferent administrator, there is only one among them, namely Omar II, who was a serious, even saintly ruler; somewhat narrow-minded it is true, but just and merciful even to his enemies. The others, Soliman, Yazid II, Walid II, were men of artistic temperament, and given to pleasure. Their reigns aroused discontent among their subjects, and accelerated the decadence of their dynasy, in spite of the important conquests achieved by their generals.

As a matter of fact, the expansion of Islam which was arrested for a time under Ali, was resumed with vigour under the Omayyads. Moawiya had organised the fleet, and there were many expeditions on land against both East and West. It could be said that the Omayyad Dynasty had taken the part of the Sasanians in its wars against the Byzantine Empire. In the East, Arabs reached Herat as early as 661, from where they went as far as Indus, traversing Afghanistan. From 674 onwards they made incursions into Transoxiana, which country they annexed in 771. In the interval they occupied Armenia, but without succeeding in conquering Anatolia. In less than forty years, Islam had reached its ultimate limits in the Orient: it stretched to the boundaries of China, and to the valley of the Indus.

The Arab conquests in the West were not less important. The Berber tribes of North Africa were at that time independent of Byzantine control. They consisted of three principal groups: the Lowata, composed of the Djerid and Auras who lived in the East of the Tripolitan country; the Sanhadja on the West composed notably of the Kotama, the Kabylia, the Masmuda of the Moroccan coast, and the veiled Sanhadja of the Sahara; and Zenata nomads, certain tribes of which lived in the Tlemcen region. Here also it was that hostility between the Sanhadja and the

Zenata which made them play into the hands of their Arab invaders. In Ifrikiya, the eastern section of North Africa (the name Maghrib covers the western section of North Africa in particular) the first two campaigns were nothing more than razzias in which the Arabs met the Byzantines, but it was for the purpose of restraining the Berbers that the Arab chief, Oqba, founded Kairawan, the headquarters of the invaders, in 670. The same chief, after an extraordinary cavalry raid which halted only at the Moroccan coast, fell into an ambuscade. Finally, in 697, at a time when the political situation seemed stabilised, the Caliph Abd-al-Malik sent a strong expedition. Carthage was taken and sacked. Though retrieved for a time by the Byzantines, they had to abandon it a year later; and it was on this occasion that the Berbers organised their resistance under Kahina, who became a more or less legendary chief. Once more disunion among the Berbers served the Arabs, and they were able to add a religious conquest to a military one. Within a few years' time the Berbers were Islamised, mostly lured by spoils. Later, they became the strongest auxiliaries of the Arabs in their conquest of Spain. After venturing into south Morocco the Arabs took Tangiers, and a little later the Balearic Islands.

Under the Visigoth occupation Spain was Christian only in name. The people, suffering from the domination of the feudal lords and bishops, were ready to welcome any invaders as liberators, and as such the Arabs appeared to them. Both slaves and serfs bought their liberation at the price of conversion to Islam. This state of affairs naturally facilitated the work of the conquerors. The Christian infantry were defeated by the Arab cavalry, and the taking of Toledo in 712 brought the Gothic domination of Spain to an end.

From 712 onwards, the Arabs began to carry their incursions beyond the Pyrenees. The Merovingian Monarchy was in an agonising state north of the Pyrenees, just as the Gothic Monarchy had been on the south banks. The Arabs came to a halt on the banks of the river Garonne, and directed their forces towards the Rhone valley, which they ravaged in 725. Seven years later their cavalry crossed Gascony, captured Bordeaux, and advanced on Poitiers. Here they were defeated by Charles Martel in 737, exactly a century after Muhammed's death, and they retired towards the south of Narbonne in disorder.

In spite of this repulse which arrested the military expansion of the Arabs, their Empire had now reached the apogee of its power. It extended from the Atlantic to the Indus, from the Caspian to the cataracts of the Nile. Nevertheless the zenith of the political power of the Omayyad Dynasty had preceded the period of its greatest territorial expansion by a few years. The power of the Omayyad Dynasty reached its height with Abd-al-Malik, at the end of the 7th century.

The Omayyads excelled primarily in their centralising ability. Just as Muhammed had succeeded in assimilating divergent elements into a single community, so the Omayyads succeeded in amalgamating into an immense Empire divers peoples and creeds which had till then never ceased to fight against each other. It was with them that the idea of the Islamic State became a reality. This kind of achievement can be realised by a liberalism which is political, religious and intellectual at the same time; and this liberalism was a characteristic of the policy of the Omayyad family, and had always been a part of their nature. Abu-Sofyan, their ancestor, had lived on friendly terms with the Christians and the Jews: his descendants had married Christians, and they had patronised orators and poets, who were still attached to pagan traditions. This patronage had included musicians and singers of both sexes. Unconsciously, the Omayyads abandoned themselves to the civilising spell of Ancient Syria. Their liberalism, however, did not make the common people forget that they were supposed to be representatives of a religion. The Omayyads scandalised those believers who had remained faithful to the austerity and the simplicity of the early days of Islam. The sombre Medina of those days censured Damascus, just as Geneva censured the Rome of the 16th century.

On the other hand, politically speaking, if Medina was the seat of an Arab state, Damascus was the capital of a Muslem empire. But this Empire had become too vast and too heterogeneous for an enduring unity. The more its frontiers stretched out, the more disproportionate the huge mass of the conquered peoples became, in comparison with the small number of the conquerors. Furthermore, the Omayyads, seeing that conversions to Islam diminished the revenue from taxes, began to put obstacles to these conversions.[1] The misrule and the superior attitude of Omayyad agents towards those nations who were the heirs to old civilisations, roused their resentment and made them remember their former days—the nationalist movements of Shubism were one of the

[1] See page 85.

results. Finally Kharidjite and Shi'ite agitation complicated an already troubled state. It was the able and active propaganda of these two factions which eventually overthrew the Omayyad Dynasty.

The Shi'ite propaganda had really begun after the death of the pious Caliph, Omar II, in 720. The Shi'ites realised that, as usual, they had been too late to profit by it themselves, and that Ali'ite agents must work for others. The descendants of Abas,[1] Muhammed's uncle, had won the respect of the believers by the dignity of their personal lives. The opposing party which by now was weakening the power of the Omayyads began to contemplate their overthrow in favour of the Abassids.

Syria sent faithful agents into the different regions to spread propaganda in favour of the Abassids. They found a favourable reception, specially in Khorasan, where there were many groups of Persians who had always felt themselves superior to the Arabs, and had never resigned themselves to subjection. Further, the unexpected help from the Shi'ites strengthened their cause. The attitude of the Shi'ites on this issue can be explained as follows: Those who held to the legitimacy of Ali's family were trying to obtain power for his descendants, and were consequently on the lookout for allies. Also, the disunion among the Shi'ites themselves served the Abassid cause. As a matter of fact, the Shi'ites were divided into parties: Imamites—these wanted Husain's son as Caliph, and withheld themselves from Abassid propaganda; and Hashimites, who were the partisans of Husain's half-brother, who was called the son of the Hanifite. When Husain died, the Hashimites nominated his

[1] See page 37.

son as their candidate, and he was called Abu-Hashim, from whom the name of the party is derived. But Abu-Hashim died in 716—probably being poisoned—leaving his rights to the great grand-son of Abas, Muhammed-ibn-Ali. As a result of this the Hashimite section of the Shi'ites became instrumental to Abassid propaganda. They continued to work in favour of the Abassids even after Muhammed-ibn-Ali's death. The two sons of Muhammed were to gather the fruit of Shi'ite propaganda which became very effective owing to one of their most powerful agents, an able and energetic man of Persian origin, known as Abu-Muslim. In 747 the black standards of the Abassids arose to defy the white standards of the Omayyads. Two years later, the first Abassid Caliph was proclaimed in Kufa, while the last Omayyad was definitely defeated. The members of his family were hunted down and exterminated in a ruthless manner. One of them escaped to Spain, where he was to found a dynasty in 754.

THE ABASSIDS. The Abassid Dynasty reigned for five centuries (750-1258). The Omayyads had been the artisans of Arab Hegemony; the Abassid Dynasty—two members of which had Persian mothers—was more Muslem than Arab. As they owed their power partly to the Persians, they were obliged to keep a balance between Persians and Arabs. It was a difficult feat, but the genius of Mansur succeeded in achieving it during the fifty years of his reign, though he was helped by a line of able ministers of Persian origin known as Barmecides. Nevertheless civil war eventually broke out between the sons of Harun-ar-Rashid, one being supported by the Arabs, and the other by the Persians. The latter won the day, but it was a breach which was never repaired.

Owing to Persian influence the Abassids moved their capital from Damascus to Bagdad, a change which inevitably affected the character of the government. The Abassid Caliphate took on many of the characteristics of the Sasanian Monarchy. Persian influence did not show itself only in the court etiquette and dresses, but in art and literature as well.

Persian influence however was not the only foreign element. The Abassid civilisation was essentially composite. The documents we have in hand from up to the advent of the Abassids present Arabic literature as being exclusively poetic and oratorical. Owing to the liberalism of the Abassid Caliphs, the intellectuals of the conquered peoples came into contact with Arabs. Ancient Greek science which had taken refuge in monasteries or schools now came into the light. The extensive influence of Hellenism in Asia after the campaign of Alexander is already well known. From the 4th century onward philosophical works of ancient Greek scholars had been translated into Syriac by Nestorians, and studied throughout Syria and Mesopotamia. On the other hand Indian influence was also making itself felt through the Iranian communities in Bactria and Soghdian (Afghanistan) who were in contact with Buddhists.

Elements of Aramean, Hindu, and Hellenic thought spread rapidly among Arabs, owing to the works of translators who played a most important part in the 8th and 9th centuries. As to Persian influence, it was less profound than is generally supposed by those who speak of Aryan reaction against Semitic genius; though it is true that Persian influence was particularly felt in poetry which quite changed its character. To those Arabs who were as yet unacquainted with the subtleties of reasoning, Arabised Persians taught the sublimity of the sciences and the power of dialectics. Briefly the part of the Persian was that of an adaptor. In Bagdad culture underwent a Renaissance which was comparable to ours of the 16th century; and the Persians affected it much as did the Italians who migrated to France during the reign of Francis I.

Contemporary with this intellectual ferment were also economic developments. Bagdad was a link between the Occident and the Far East, and she had commercial houses in India, and even in China; but these commercial relations did not necessarily lead to religious conversion. The conversion of Madagascar to Islam, due to the emigration of Arabs from the Persian Gulf, proceeded apace from the 8th to the 9th century, but the Islamisation of the Indian Archipelago and parts of China were of a much later date. In the Indian Archipelago, it was only towards the latter half of the 13th century that Islam gained a foothold in Sumatra and began to oust Hinduism, which it had eliminated by the 17th century. In China, it was after the defeat of the Thang Emperors by the Arabs on the Talas River in 751 that Islam began to penetrate. That defeat is one of the decisive battles of history, and was due to the Emperors hiring Arab mercenaries to fight their own rebellious subjects.

Of the five centuries of the Abassid dynasty it is only the first which was one of grandeur and great prosperity. It covers the reigns of Mansur, Harun-ar-Rashid and Mamun. Renan speaks of the time as an era which "the world will dream of forever." The inherent weakness of the dynasty manifested itself immediately after the first of its rule. The Empire had become too vast, and signs of disintegration began to be evident. In face of this, the Caliph felt his temporal power passing from him, and as a result he began to lay more emphasis on his spiritual power, a policy which naturally led to reactions and religious intolerance. Furthermore, the Caliph, from early times, had divided his subjects in order to rule them. He had no confidence either in the Arabs or in the Arabised Persians; and the Kharidjites, and the Shi'-ites were continually rising against him. To protect himself, he formed a special body-guard of Turkish mercenaries gathered from among those with whom the Arabs had come into contact in Central Asia. These mercenaries, like those of Carthage and of Byzantium, acquired a dominant position. By the middle of the 10th century, the Caliph had lost all his effective power, and had become nothing more than one of the "Faineant" kings whose "Amir-al-Umera" (Amirs-in-Chief) reminded one of the "Maires du Palais" of the Merovingians. These Amirs-in-Chief were appointed sometimes from among the Persians, and sometimes from among the Turks.

This weakness very soon brought about a political decentralisation. From 755 onward, Spain remained loyal to the last Omayyad who had escaped from Abassid persecution. Since that fugitive Prince had reconciled the conflicting aims of different parties, Arab, Berber or native, the Kingdom of Cordova had faced several changes of fortune. It had in turn to hold its own against Christian invasions and international dissensions. But in 912, there appeared in Spain a great ruler under the name of Abdurrahman III, who conquered the provinces lost by his predecessors, established political unity, reformed the state finance, and took the title of Caliph in 929. Under the rule of Hakam II, who was a great patron of art and learning, Cordova became a rival to Bagdad. The tenth century was for Muslem Spain an era of incomparable brilliance; but its splendour had no morrow, for beginning with the last years of the same century, decline set in and was hastened because of internal rivalries, Christian raids and religious intolerance. A minister of genius, Ibn-Abi-Amir Mansur (Almanzur of the Western historians) struggled in vain to maintain the political unity of Spain. A little while after his death, that is in the first years of the eleventh century, Spain was divided into a half a dozen small states which could not successfully resist Christian invasion.

Even before the Abassid reign however, the Berbers of Africa were once more carried away by their love of religious novelties, and abandoned Orthodox Islam for heretical doctrines of Kharidjism.[1] These doctrines reminded them of those Circoncellions[2] and satisfied their democratic instincts. The Kharidjite Movement, which was national as well as religious, spread from Morocco in 740, and gained the whole of North Africa, as well as a part of Spain. The Abassids tried in vain to prevent the birth of autonomous little states in spite of bloody struggles. Ta-

[1] See pages 58 and 177.

[2] A Christian sect in North Africa known as Circoncellions. They followed the teaching of Donatus, the Bishop of Carthage, who had discussed the efficiency of Sacrament administered by certain Bishops. He had thus attacked not the doctrine itself but the discipline of the Christian Church.

hart, a model of Kharidjite principality, was reigned over by the Rustamid dynasty; at Sidjilmasa there were the Midrarids; at Tlemcen the Banu Ifren dynasty ruled, and at Fas the Idrisids. The rest of North Africa did not take long to free itself from Abassid rule. From 800 onwards the Abassid Caliph had conferred the province of Ifrikiya (Tunis and a part of Constantine) on its governor as a hereditary fief, in return for an annual tribute. It was really renunciation in disguise. That governor (and the dynasty he founded under the name of Aghlabids), found an outlet to the surplus energy of his subjects by sending fleets to the Italian, Corsican and Sardinian coasts. These Arab forces took fifty years to conquer Sicily, which was the land of an age-old civilisation where Greek, Roman and Oriental genius met and harmonised Muslem and Christian aspirations and aims.

In Egypt in the 8th century, the Tulunids, governors who were practically independent, prepared the way for the Ikshidid and Fatimid Dynasties. And when the last two eventually came into power it was no longer merely the political power of the Caliph which suffered an eclipse, but his religious power as well. Just as it had been in the case of the Abassids, a veritable army of secret agents brought these two dynasties into power. Just as the Abassids had used Shi'ite help, so the Fatimids used the services of one of the sects derived from Shi'ism. Fatimid origins are uncertain, but they pretended to be the descendants of Fatima and Ali. The heroic character of their early adventures, their energy and the rapidity with which they overthrew the Abassids and conquered North Africa, and their establishment of a Caliphate in Cairo fifty years later with heretical tendencies, made them dangerous rivals of the Abassids and conferred on them a mysterious prestige. It will be seen later in the fifth chapter, what influence this Dynasty had on the religious evolution of Islam.

About twenty years earlier, Idris—this time an incontestable descendant—introduced Shi'ism into Morocco and founded a Dynasty. But the Idrissid branch of Shi'ism was confined to the Maghreb only. Under Fatimids the whole of North Africa became Shi'ite just as it had become Kharidjite at an earlier date. A missionary named Abu-Abd-Allah, in connivance with the Berbers residing in Mecca, laid the foundations for Fatimid power, just as Abu-Muslim had done for the Abassids. And just as had been the case of Abu-Muslem Abu-Abd-Allah had to pay with his life for the jealousy and suspicion which his great influence roused in the master whose cause he served so faithfully. Obaidullah, the said master, was one whom the Abassids had expelled from Egypt, and who came to Maghreb in search of fortune where he was thrown into prison by the Midrarid prince in Sidjilmasa. The faithful Abu-Abd-Allah had then come to the rescue. He overthrew the Aghlabids, expelled the Rustamid Dynasty from Tahart, and placed his master Obaid-Allah on the Aghlabid throne in Tunis in 910. For a few years after this, North Africa became the scene of a ferocious struggle between Kharidjism and Shi'ism. The latter won the day in about 960. This religious and political conflict involved Berber tribes: the Kotama and the Sanhudja fought for the Fatimids against the Zenata, the partisans of the Omayyad Caliph in Cordova. The conflict is reminiscent of the wars between Lakhmids, the auxiliaries of the Persians, and the Ghassanids, the auxiliaries of the Byzantine Empire.

The Fatimids, now masters in the Muslem West, turned their attention to the East. In 969, Egypt, which had withstood their previous attacks, was now captured without much difficulty. Shi'ism became at least the official religion for two centuries. This conquest naturally changed the centre of the Fatimid Empire. Leaving their faithful Sanhadja Berbers to guard North Africa, they turned to the conquest of Syria. But their power in Syria vacillated until the Seljukid Turks conquered Syria in 1076, and drove out the Fatimids.[1]

At the end of the 10th century the Fatimid Empire comprised Egypt, Syria, the islands of the Mediterranean, and North Africa down to the Atlantic Ocean. But it was only for a short time for North Africa soon threw off the Fatimid yoke just as it had overthrown the domination of the Abassids. The transference of the Fatimid capital from Tunis to Cairo had done much to relax its hold over the Berber princes. From 972 onwards, Fatimid lieutenant in Tunis rejected his suzerainty and founded the Dynasty of the Zirids. Another dynasty, that of the Hammadids established itself in Algeria in the Bougie region in 1007. In the West, the Berber tribes were disputing what remained of Idrissid power. About the same period Muslem Spain was being divided into regional kingdoms called Reyes of Taifas.

The Hillalian invasion, an event, the political and economic consequences of which cannot be exaggerated, struck the final blow at North Africa. Towards 1050, the Fatimid Caliph in Egypt, seeing

[1] See page 228.

the Zirids abandon Shi'ism in favour of Orthodox Islam, dispersed westward the undisciplined and looting Arab tribes of Banu-Hillal and Sulaim. They had emigrated from Arabia into Egypt and had settled in Upper Egypt where they had become a nuisance. These tribes now ravaged the Tripolitan country for two years, after which they entered Tunis. The Zirids and the Hammadids could not unite, and their separate attempts to stop the invasion were in vain. The Tunisian towns became prey to adventurers who at times established local principalities. The rise of Tunis to fortune was brought about by the Bani-Khorasan, one of these adventurer dynasties. The helpless Zirids withdrew to one of their own cities; the Hammadids, whose days were also numbered, did the same in the beginning of the 12th century. Then in 1148 the Normans of Sicily, now masters of the Mediterranean, expelled them both from their last refuge. Up to that time the Arabs had been an oligarchy amid Berber masses. The Hillalian invasions increased their numbers, but it also aggravated the religious and the political conflicts, and destroyed the economic prosperity of North Africa, which, for centuries afterwards remained static.

Let us now retreat a century and consider the Orient where another struggle was going on. While the Berbers of North Africa were struggling against the Arab Hegemony, the same Hegemony was trying to defend itself on the extreme edge of the Muslem world, against a peril which increased daily—the Turks. An age-old struggle of Iran against Turan which had been suspended for a time, had broken out again. It had begun at a time when the Sasanids, who held the commercial route of the Far East against Byzantium, were also defending their frontiers against the Ephtalites of Turkestan, and against the Turks from Altai. This old rôle of Margraves, as keepers of the frontiers of civilisation, was taken from the tenth century onward by the local dynasties of the Orient in Persia. The first rulers of the Tahirid and Saffarid dynasties, who had become independent of Bagdad as early as the 9th century, were the condottieri who conquered for themselves domains in Khorasan, Seistan and Fars. But owing to the Samanid influence, the sentiment of national unity among Persians was reborn. The Samanids, from the vantage point of their Transoxanian fiefs, could carry the war down into the Kirghiz plains, and once peace was established in the East, could conquer the whole of Eastern Persia. In Khorasan and Transoxania, several towns became centres of art and intellectual achievement, where the use of the Arab language did not prevent the blossoming out of Persian literature—the Samanid Dynasty's eternal title to glory.

Meanwhile in the East of Iran, the Buid (Persian) Dynasty also rose rapidly to power. For fifteen years the governors of provinces occupying Western Persia had brought Shi'ism with them into these regions, and had finally established themselves in Bagdad at the court of the Caliph and ruled there in his name. Thus began the struggle for supremacy between the Buids and the Samanids which lasted for half a century. The Samanid princes, worn out by war, and reduced to the necessity of defending themselves against a turbulent military aristocracy, followed the example of the Caliphs of Bagdad—that is, they engaged Turkish mercenaries. This dangerous practice of engaging alien mercenaries, analogous to the use of Swiss mercenaries by European monarchies, was very prevalent in Islam from the earliest times. The rulers of Mecca employed the Abyssinians, and Bagdad and Cairo the Turks, Berbers and Negroes; and in each case rivalries between these mercenaries led to many bloody conflicts. On this occasion one of the Turkish mercenaries, an old slave, received the governorship of Khorasan from the Samanids. Dismissed, he crossed the Afghan mountains and laid down the foundations of an Empire in Ghazna. It was the death-knell of the Samanids. In 999, the last Samanid prince was driven out from Khorasan by Mahmud, the strong man representing the new dynasty of the Ghaznevids.

Mahmud, towards the end of his reign had conquered not only Eastern Persia, but also a part of India, where he introduced Islam. Fervently Orthodox, he requested his investiture of the Caliph in Bagdad. But though he constituted himself the champion of Islam against the Turks of Kashgar and the Seljukids who threatened his frontiers, he was only able to delay, not to prevent a fatal invasion by others of his own race.[1] Fortunately the Persian civilisation in due course harmonised all these divers elements: *Persia capta ferum victorem capiet.*

Hence about the middle of the 11th century, the Muslem world was disorganized. It was religiously disorganised, for Orthodox Muslems were obliged to defend themselves on one side in Iraq and Egypt against Shi'ism which was still formidable, and on the other side, against the progress of the Christians in Spain. It was politically disorganised, because the

[1] See Chap. VI.

Muslem world was broken into small kingdoms, and not one of them was strong enough to impose its hegemony upon the others. But on the extreme borders of this worn-out world new forces were entering the field of action. The Seljukid Turks drove out the Buids from Bagdad in 1055, and re-established political and religious unity in the East. The Almoravids, coming from the Sahara, achieved the same temporarily in the West. Thus, after five centuries of Arab hegemony, a period of great invasions began, and changed the centre of gravity of Islam.[1] Before considering the new era which followed, it would be useful to recapitulate the general characteristics of the first period.

CONDITIONS OF ARAB EXPANSION. The conquests of Islam were facilitated by several factors already in existence.

In the first place, the ground was often prepared by the internal dissensions. We have seen the Arabs welcomed by the Egyptian Copts and by the Syrians almost as saviours. Similarly, in Persia and in Spain the existing governments had already alienated their subjects by misrule. Nevertheless the Arabs softened rather than abolished these troublesome administrations. They retained the officials of the country in their former posts, especially those of the financial departments who might continue to collect taxes, but in the name of Islam and so assure a revenue which was the only means of maintaining the fidelity of the Caliph's army.

A second factor was the free initiative accorded to military commanders, even by the most authoritative Caliphs. Under the reign of Othman and several

[1] See Chap. VI.

others of the Omayyads, conquests were carried on almost automatically, without any intervention on the part of the Caliph.

Quite a number of these commanders, at least in the early days of Islam, were inspired by a sincere faith. But it would be difficult to assert that none of them, especially after Omar's Caliphate, had any personal ambitions. Was Moawiya, for example, really disinterested in his Syrian Campaign? Did not Amr contemplate the possibility of gaining for himself a principality when he so abruptly attacked Egypt? Similar questions arise with regard to others, especially the conquerors of North Africa and Spain.

But those commanders, even when they had a personal ambition, were followed on their campaigns by ignorant and sturdy soldiers, the majority of whom believed firmly in the promise of the Sacred Book that those who die for their faith would attain eternal felicity. This was an element of inestimable importance as giving a moral force to the combatants, and also, of course, giving the commanders an absolute authority. Naturally this did not completely exclude pecuniary motives for those who found in pillage and looting an opportunity to satisfy instincts and habits inherited from their pagan days.

Finally, these wars were not as improvised as they might seem to have been. We have seen how the Arabs took advantage of the disunion and momentary weakness of their adversaries, as for example, on the Syrian frontier. But the Arab bands were neither without experience nor discipline. The beginnings of a military tradition, more or less stable, are found already among those whose fathers had fought in the Lakhmid or Ghassanid ranks against the old armies of Persia or Byzantium.[1] There was also the possibility of the Caliphs sending their subjects on expedition in order to keep them away from the capital, and also strengthen their loyalty to Islam by giving them conquests and spoils.

THE HOLY WAR (JIHAD) AND THE ADMINISTRATION OF THE CONQUERED LANDS. The propagation of Islam by the sword was a religious duty, and any war which had for its aims the bringing of men to the true religion was just. This idea had become one of the fundamental motive forces of Islam. For though on the one hand, the Koran recommends that men should be brought to true religion by wisdom and gentle counsel,[2] elsewhere the Koran commands that true-believers shall fight all those infidels who deny or stand in the way of the One God (2:244). It might seem that Muhammed himself was not clear in his mind about the consequences of the Holy War. Nevertheless the conception which eventually influenced Islam was that of continual warfare between Muslems and non-Muslems, and this from a short time after Muhammed's death. Theoretically, Holy War was considered a duty for every free and able-bodied male Muslem, who also had the means to take part in it. The duty was not rigorously imposed, for, if a certain number of Muslems were engaged in the Holy War the rest were exempt from it.

What then were the rules of the Holy War? It was obligatory to fight against the people of the neigh-

[1] See page 20.

[2] "Call to the Way of your Lord with wisdom and goodly exhortation and have disputations with them in the best manner" (Chap. 16:126).

bouring non-Muslem territories of Islam. That is to say, the territories of war (dar-al-harb) must be transferred into territories of Islam (dar-al-Islam). Between these two extremes came the tributary lands conquered by peaceful means; that is by treaty (dar-as-Sulh). This third category became subject first to persuasive methods.

Before any hostile act could be committed, the infidels must be asked to embrace Islam. If they accepted, they became henceforth a part of the Muslem community (Umma), and had the same rights as the other Muslems. But their apostasy was punishable by death.

If they refused there were two ways of treating them: either to decide the issue by a resort to arms, or by compelling them to pay a tax which would also ensure them Muslem protection. The former was known as Anwa, that is to say, conquest by force; the latter as Sulh, that is to say, conquest by capitulation, or peaceful means.

In the first case (conquest by force) a distinction was established in early times between two kinds of property which fell into the hands of the conquerors. First, the personal property which fell into the hands of the fighters on the battlefield; and, second, the real estate, which fell into the hands of the conquerors as a result of conquest. The former was called Ghanima, and the latter Fai. Of the Ghanima, four-fifths were divided between the fighters, the cavalry receiving one share more than the infantry. The remaining fifth was the "Share of God" according to a verse given by a revelation a little after the Battle of Badr: "And know that whatever thing you acquire in war, a fifth of it is for Allah and for the Apostle and for the near of kin and orphans and the needy and the wayfarer. . . ."[1] Prisoners of war were classified as Ghanima. They belonged to the chief of the Muslem community (the Imam), and he could keep them as slaves, liberate them, or kill them.

In the second case (conquest by Treaty) Muhammed himself made a distinction between those peoples who were possessors of revealed Books and those who had no revealed Books, and were idol-worshippers. Christians and Jews were considered as people who had a sacred Book (Ahl-al-Kitab); and then those who believed in one of the prophets were privileged, though their books were abrogated in the Koran. This was clearly expressed in the Koran: "And the followers of the Gospel must judge by what Allah has revealed in it; and whoever had not judged by what Allah revealed, those are the transgressors (infidels)."[2] Hence Christians and Jews, after their submission, were free in the exercise of their religion, but they had to pay a tax. To the class of people of a sacred Book, others besides Christians and Jews were admitted in early times: such as the Zoroastrians whom Muslems met at Behrein and the Samaritans of Palestine. While, under the reign of Caliph Mamun in the 9th century, the Sabaens of Harran, who succeeded in passing themselves off as the Sabaens of legend, mentioned in the Koran, were also allowed freedom for their cult, the same as the Christians and the Jews.[3] "Surely, those who believe and those who are Jews, and Christians, and the Sabaeans, whosoever believed in Allah and the Judgment Day and does good, they shall have

[1] Chap. 8:41.
[2] Chap. 5:47.
[3] Chap. 2:62.

their reward from their Lord. . . ." Later in the 14th century this tolerance was extended to the Chinese. All these protected peoples were called the people of the contract or of obligation (Ahl-al-Dhimma or simply Dhimmis).

The second category of the conquered comprised all those non-Muslems, who were not Dhimmis and were called materialists (Dahri) or heathens. In theory they were to be given the choice between conversion and death, but in practice this distinction disappeared very early. The term Dhimmis (the people of the Contract) was applied to all those who submitted and accepted the obligations, as in the case of Indian idol-worshippers. What were those obligations?

In return for freedom to exercise their cult, the male inhabitants of the conquered country paid a poll-tax called Djizya, the tax of tolerance mentioned in the Koran. "Fight those who do not believe in Allah . . . until they pay the tax in acknowledgment of superiority. . . ."[1] The exact sum to be paid was fixed by treaty. Women, children, old men, in brief, non-combatants, were exempt. Slaves and poor monks were also exempt. This tax was to be paid in cash, and could also be paid in kind, but wine, dead animals were not accepted. For insolvents there was no corporal punishment, but there was a term of imprisonment.

On the other hand the Dhimmis who preserved the freehold of their real estate or enjoyed the use, cultivation and rent of lands, paid a tax for the privilege. This was called Kharadj, probably from the Greek word Khoregya. This tax already existed in the

[1] Chap. 9:29.

regions under Persian or Byzantine domination. Muslem tax-collectors collected both in kind and in money.

The Dhimmis were subject to certain other obligations and restraints as follows: contribution to the upkeep of Muslem armies; particular dress to distinguish them from others, known as the sign of Ghiyar; interdiction to ride horses or to carry arms; interdiction to build new edifices of culture in addition to those accepted by the conquerors; interdiction to be too ostentatious in their rites; invalidity of their evidence in a court of law; indemnity in case of murder instead of Talion. In return for these concessions they enjoyed like any Muslem the protection of the law for their persons and their property.

The terms used for the two taxes, Djizya and Kharadj, were confused with each other in the very early days of Islam; but a definite distinction between them was established in Omar's time. Kharadj designated the land tax, or tax paid on estate. It was the revenue from this particular tax which supplied most of the funds for the Public Treasury after the great conquests under Omar. The spoils of the battlefield were divided between the fighters by Omar himself. But partly for the purpose of creating taxes, partly for preventing the fighters from neglecting their lands, Omar left all the arable land to its original owners in return for a tax which was to be paid even in cases of conversion to Islam. This last clause brought about the disappearance of Kharadj. For, with time conversions multiplied and the converts paid the same tax as the Arab Muslem conquerors. We have already seen that with the exception of the pious Omar II, the Omayyad Caliphs did not favour conversions in general; for especially when these conversions were among the owners of arable land, they were due to self-interest. Further, they diminished the land-tax. From the time of Othman to Moawiya the revenue from Egypt had fallen to half of what it was when the Copts embraced Islam.

The principles of the Public Treasury (bait-al-mal) were established in Muhammed's time. Registers of birth, marriage and death were established, and the respective rights of Muslems to the benefits of war were fixed according to the seniority, and importance of their genealogy. Fiscal administration was considerably extended—this was the social revolution which was among the principal causes of Othman's assassination. In brief, the "share of Allah" (mal-al-Allah) transformed itself rapidly into communal property, under the name of "mal-al-Muslimin." Further, under the Byzantine and Persian influences the organisation of the Public Treasury went through a further evolution.

In theory the Public Treasury was administered by the Imam (the spiritual and temporal chief of the Muslem community), or by his representative. The sources of revenue were: Djizya (poll-tax) and Kharadj (tax on real estate and land) paid by Dhimmis; Zakat (the poor rate) a legal alms which Muslems were obliged to pay, which was also called ochr (dime) when it was the land-tax paid by Muslems on the land (this land being the Imam's, rented to cultivators); and two other adventitious taxes paid by Muslems: the Khoms (one-fifth) on the exploitation of mines, discovered treasure, etc. and the inheritance tax on the property of those who left no male issue.

It will be seen on page 154 how Zakat and Khoms were used according to rules laid down for them; or at least, in theory.

These taxes were levied by the provincial governors, quite a number of whom were originally the commanders of regional forces. The wide extent of conquests necessitated organised military centres in different parts of the Empire. The Muslem historian Masudi, in one of his works enumerates seven such metropoles, called Amsar: Basra, founded in the beginning of the Persian conquest towards 635, as well as Kufa; Fostat (Old Cairo) about 640; Ramleh of Palestine, and Wasit of Iraq, in the early part of the 8th century; Bagdad, founded about 762 by the Abassid Caliph Mansur; Samara, founded about 835 by Motasim, of whom Masudi says that he was the first Caliph to engage Turkish mercenaries, and was forced to leave Bagdad because the inhabitants objected to the presence of these aliens. Seven Caliphs lived in Samara (the Avignon of the Caliphate), a city which is important for the study of Islamic art.

In certain regions, especially those captured from the Byzantines, the military organisations were not changed. In Syria, for example, there were five divisions (djond, legion) in imitation of the Byzantine system, which included Palestine, Jordan, Damascus, Homs and Kinnasrine. In the same way, Harun-ar-Rashid organised a djond in Cilicia.

ADMINISTRATIVE ORGANISATIONS. The command of the Holy War and the organisation of the land tenure in conquered regions were defined as belonging to the Caliph.

The Caliph had to be a member of the tribe of Kureish. He was absolute head. To rise against him was equivalent to rising against God. He was elected; or at least, he was in theory. Traces of this tradition were evident at the time of the hereditary Caliphate, in the oath of allegiance (bai'a) taken at the coronation of a new Caliph. In brief, the Caliph was the representative (naib) of the Prophet, and the depositary of Law (Shari'a) inspired by God.

In the reign of Omar, the title of Caliph (Khalifa Rasul Allah) meaning the Lieutenant of the Messenger of God, was given to the spiritual and temporal chief of the Muslem community.[1] To the high dignity of the successor of the Prophet, two other titles and duties were added: Commander of the Believers (Amir-al-Muminin) which was adopted by Omar; and the title of Imam which meant presiding over public prayers. The Omayyads were more Amir-al-Muminin than Imam. Nevertheless several among them did preside over public prayers in person. But on the whole the study of the religious Law was confined to Medina in their time. But with Abassids the centre for the study of the Religious Law changed from Medina to Bagdad. The Omayyad Caliph was above all a chief of state; Abassid was a pontiff-monarch, who wore the Prophet's mantle and who never missed an occasion in which he could officially affirm his relationship to the Prophet. But as this sublime rank isolated the Caliph from his subjects, as well as from the administrative, the latter therefore developed with a certain freedom. The Diwans[2] were primarily registers of accounts kept in Greek, in Syria, and Egypt, and in Pehlevi in Persia; they

[1] Later the title Caliph extended to the chiefs of religious Brotherhoods, and even to the officials in Morocco.

[2] Plural Dawawin—the French word Douane is derived from it.

were from Abd-al-Malik's time onward kept in Arabic. The term Diwan designated under the Abassids the finance, land administration departments, chancelleries and other such offices of state. Between all these divers organisations and the rulers there had to be an intermediary—it was the Vezir. The Institution of the Vezir carried in itself a germ of decay. The Caliph who left everything in the hands of his Vezir gradually lost the habit of power. The first scribe (katib) as intermediary between the Caliph and the state departments to obtain the prerogatives of a prime minister was Khalid. He became the first of that famous line of prime ministers, the Barmecides, who governed under Caliph Mansur. Yahya, the son of Khalid, became Harun-ar-Rashid's prime minister with unlimited powers, and it was he who in effect governed the Empire for seventeen years.

Nevertheless one must not believe in a systematic centralisation. Provinces had a large autonomy in matters of finance and civil administration, which was rendered easy by the amelioration of the postal system under the Omayyads. The principle of this postal system was taken from the Byzantines and the Persians. The directors of Posts were nominated either by the Caliph or by the Vezir. These directors eventually became agents of information for the central government, and therefore were regarded with distrust by provincial governors.

It was not only the administration which profited from these postal services; they were also advantageous to commercial relations. Under the Abassids, Basra became, not only a centre of theological and philological activity, but a commercial capital as well. It imported the products of the Far East, silks, spices, ebony and ivory, and exported glass-ware, dates, arms, textiles, rugs, jewelry to the West. As for maritime commerce, we have already seen Aghlabids [1] in the Mediterranean. In the 11th century, the fleets of the Omayyads of Spain had their harbours on the French coasts, just as the Aghlabids had theirs on the Italian coasts. In the eastern Mediterranean, the Arabs after ousting the Byzantines, themselves became intermediaries between Europe and Asia, and masters of a commerce which only became paralyzed because of their ethnic and political divisions.

Meanwhile the police created by the Omayyads developed at the same time as the Empire. To the prefect of police, called Sahib-ach-Chorta,[2] meaning the commander of the guard, the inspector (Muhtasab) was added, who was charged to watch over public morals, and over weights and measures.[3]

Finally, just as the Caliph delegated the provincial Imam to preside over public prayers in his name, he also delegated the Cadi to carry out his judicial power. Sometimes these two functions were both performed by the governor of the province, and sometimes different persons were appointed directly by the Caliph to these posts. The Cadi had to be upright and educated, possessing a profound knowledge of the law, which he was called upon to apply.[4] Besides settling law cases, he had to administer the property of minors and the unfit, mortmain property in general, and in fact, was responsible for discharging practically all litigation in civil and penal matters.

1 See page 72.
2 This name was changed to Wali later.
3 In the 83d chapter of the Koran those who defraud are cursed.
4 See page 116.

In Islam, it must be remembered, judicial administration always had a double aspect (Laic and Ecclesiastic), so only those affairs which were outside the Religious Law could escape the Cadi's jurisdiction. It will be now necessary to examine the foundations of the Muslem Law.

CHAPTER III

The Foundations of the Law

I. The Koran

THE Koran is the Bible of Islam. What does the word Koran mean? Muslem savants have discussed at length the pronunciation, the origin and the meaning of the word. Koran (Qor'an) is derived from the Arabic root Qara'a meaning "to read," or more generally meaning "to recite." The Koran is the revelation given to Muhammed and meant to be read or recited afterwards. The sacred book of Islam is sometimes called the "Kitab," which means "the Book" or the Scriptures; and sometimes the Dhikr, meaning "warning."

The Koran is divided into 144 chapters. A chapter in the Koran is called a "Sura" in Arabic. This word is of uncertain origin, primarily it signified "Revelation," and also means "a gathering of several revelations or fragments of revelations." In certain verses of the Koran, the unbelievers were asked to produce Chapters (Suras) of the same value as those in the Koran.[1] These verses, Allah declares to be signs (Ayat) revealed by Him[2] . . . whenever a (Sura) is revealed, "the faithful must follow their prophet in his striving in the way of Allah."[3]

[1] Chap. 2:23; Chap. 10:38.
[2] Chap. 24:v. 1.
[3] Chap. 9:v. 86.

With a view to the recitation of the Koran it was divided later into thirty parts (Djuz'), and into sixty parts known as "hizb," meaning "division."

The number of the verses of the Koran are 6211, corresponding to nearly two-thirds of the New Testament. The Koran would be shorter if repetitions were eliminated, but such repetitions are inevitable and even necessary in writing of this sort. Lane-Poole says with some justice: that "if the Jewish stories and repetitions, and temporary exhortations, and the personal revindications were set aside, Muhammed's sermons could occupy a very small space."

MUHAMMED AND REVELATION. To what origin did Muhammed attribute his revelations? He tells us that the Koran is part of a Celestial Book, the Mother of the Book.[1] That Celestial Book is accessible only to those who are pure. Of this basic book Muhammed claimed to know only certain parts, which were revealed to him in the Arabic language. As to the manner in which these revelations were made the Koran gives somewhat obscure explanations, and it is certain that Muhammed himself was not very clear about this in his mind. What is certain is that Allah spoke to him through the intermediary of a spirit whom Muhammed believes to be an angel, and calls the Angel Gabriel (Djabrail). This spirit had previously inspired Muhammed's predecessors. "He gave Jesus, the son of Mary, clear arguments, and strengthened him with the Holy Spirit."[2] For Muhammed's part, Allah commands him to tell unbelievers that: "The Holy Spirit has revealed it from your Lord, with the truth."[3]

[1] Koran, Chap. 13:39.

[2] Koran, Chap. 2:87 and 253.

[3] Koran, Chap. 16:102.

It is probable that Muhammed did not give a name immediately to the spirit which inspired him. In one of the most beautiful passages of the Koran, revealed in the first period, he describes the apparition without giving a name to it.[1] He gives a name to the Spirit, only in the last parts of the Koran.[2]

According to tradition Muhammed perceived a kind of rumbling noise, and was then seized by a strong fever; he became pale and trembling, and would ask to be enveloped in a mantle. Certain tardy historians, especially the Byzantines, have spoken of Muhammed as suffering from epilepsy. It is true that in the Orient, as well as in the Occident, epileptics were considered as being possessed of a spirit. The transports of Muhammed became more frequent after he received the first revelation, which took place in the month of Ramadan.[3] It was for this reason that this month was chosen later as the time for fasting.

Tradition affirms that in the beginning of his mission, and even before it, Muhammed multiplied his fastings and often spent the nights in prayer. If this fact—sometimes disputed—is exact his fasts may have favoured his visions, which usually happened at night, by weakening his system. One of his best known visions is his "Ascension in a Night" (Isra). While asleep, the Angel Gabriel placed him upon a fabulous horse, Borak—a kind of female Centaur—which took him to Jerusalem, Hebron and Bethlehem, where he met Abraham, Moses and Jesus. This ascension became a favourite subject for Muslem poets and illuminators. Associated with this is the miraculous

1 Koran, Chap. 53.
2 Chap. 2:97.
3 Chap. 97.

mark of his foot (Qadam sherif) on the rock of the Mosque in Jerusalem, which he made when he mounted Borak. This mark believers have discovered also in a number of places in other parts of the Muslem world.

It is evident that the Koran could not be entirely the outcome of an ecstasy, for an ecstasy of this nature presupposes a violent excitement which would permit nothing but words and isolated phrases. One may suppose that even the most ancient parts have undergone a certain amount of modification and elaboration, but it is impossible to prove it. Nevertheless the fundamental characteristic of the Koran is its fragmentary nature. This lack of composition, which is so flagrant, is due precisely to the manner in which Muhammed was inspired. If one passes from one subject to another in the Koran without any transition, it is because these revelations had their momentary impetus from the attacks of Muhammed's adversaries in Mecca, or political circumstances in Medina, or other causes. Besides, the Koran makes a clear distinction, between verses whose significance is certain, and those which can be interpreted in several ways.[1] What is more, certain revelations abrogate not only the precepts of those religions which were in existence before Islam, but also certain verses in the Koran itself which were revealed to Muhammed at an earlier date. "For whatever communication we abrogate or cause to be forgotten, We bring one better than it, or one like it."[2] In short Allah did not hesitate to come back on what He had previously prescribed. It is this particularity which gave

[1] Chap. 3:v. 6.
[2] Chap. 2:v. 106.

birth to a huge number of commentaries in regard to abrogated or abrogating verses.

Nevertheless, in the eyes of Muhammed his religion had the same source as Christianity and Judaism, all these three religions being derived from the same Celestial Book. The Koran was given to Muhammed in "plain Arabic language. And most surely from the same source as the Scriptures of the ancients." [1] The Koran confirms the Law of Moses, the Bible of Jesus, and the Psalms of David. Besides in the Koran itself,[2] tradition also presents Muhammed as an "Ummi," that is, a man who could not read and who therefore could not have read the sacred books himself. This identity of Islam with the two preceding religions he proclaimed during his stay at Mecca; but in Medina, he attenuated his previous declaration. As a matter of fact, according to those parts of the Koran revealed in this second period of his life, "the Jews and Christians have received only a part of the Holy Writ; and, what is more grave, they have altered words. Of those who are Jews, there are those who alter words from their places." [3] The influence of the sects derived from Judaism or Christianity, which were numerous in Arabia in those days, is indirectly but incontestably reflected on the Koran.

But the influence of Arab paganism which Muhammed tried to suppress is even more apparent during the first days of his mission. The very style of the Koran, formed of irregularly cadenced sentences with

1 Chap. 26:195-196.

2 In three Suras verses occur as a refrain. See the recent studies of the Bible by Père Jousse.

3 Koran, Chap. 4:46.

occasional rhymes[1] is reminiscent of the "Sadj" a form of prose-poetry where the rhyming words occur at regular intervals—a style of rhetoric which probably preceded poetry with a regular metre. But this analogy is only superficially applicable, for the true tone "sadj" demanded a rhythmic precision and harmony which one never finds in the Koran. This "sadj," which appeared very much altered at a later date in Arabic literature, was originally uttered in the language used by the pagan "kahina" of the old days. The Arab Kahin (pagan divine, or soothsayer) is often compared with the Hebrew "Kohen." But the analogy is again a superficial one. The "Kohen" arranged the sacrificial ceremonies, and was a doctor of religious science, while the Kahin was essentially a soothsayer. His rôle was an important one in the time of Arab paganism. He was consulted for all sorts of important affairs: Wars, litigations, lost or stolen goods or animals, and the detection of crime. The visions of the "Kahin" were of a maleficent nature, for it was a demon (Djinn, Shaytan) which inspired him. But Muhammed speaks of a spirit, not of a demon, as responsible for his inspiration. The "Kahin" expressed himself in a confused manner, and his oaths were in terms of natural phenomena.

In the earlier sections of the Koran there are a number of oaths of the same kind.

Rhythmic prose, the intervention of a mysterious spirit, and the prevalence of oaths, provided Muhammed's adversaries with grounds for calling him a Kahin or Sha'ir (poet). A poet was more or less the same as a soothsayer, for the pagan poet was also inspired by a demon. On the other hand, one under-

[1] Arab historians have preserved a few examples.

stands very well why Muhammed defended himself against these charges, declaring himself an enemy of poetry, though he made use of poetic forms when occasion called for them.[1]

There are some who affirm that the Koran was written in a popular form of language, and altered after Muhammed's death, but this appears unfounded if one examines it with care. As for the style of the Koran which is sometimes violent and sometimes serene, it has the characteristics of the orator rather than of the poet. This style changes according to the time the revelation was received; and it is from these variations in style that a very approximate chronology of the Suras was established. Of this we will speak later.

ESTABLISHMENT OF THE KORANIC TEXT. There was no collection of the Koranic texts when Muhammed died. It is possible that some of the earliest revelations have not been preserved. But important fragments had already been written on flat bones, palm leaves and stones. Because of the commercial importance of the Sacred Cities, a considerable number of their inhabitants knew how to read and write. Tradition tells us even the names of those who have acted as scribes to Muhammed: Obayy ben Kaab, Abdallah ben Abi-Sarh, and, above all, Zaid ben Tsabit.

The honour of collecting for the first time these dispersed fragments falls to Abu-Bekr, Muhammed's successor, or rather to Omar, who it was advised him to do this. In the 11th or the 12th year of the Hegira, quite a number of persons who had committed the Koran to memory died in the war against the false

[1] Chap. 52:29; Chap. 65:42.

prophet Musailima.[1] It was then that Omar, afraid of seeing the whole of the sacred text disappear, declared that Abu-Bekr should collect the revelations in 633. At first Abu-Bekr hesitated to undertake the task, as Muhammed had not spoken of it to him. But he finally consented, and charged the young Zaid ben Tsabit with the mission of collecting all the fragments written on different objects and the fragments remembered by the companions of Muhammed. Tsabit gathered all the existing fragments, classified and copied them on separate leaves (Sohof), and gave them to Abu-Bekr.

This first version of the Koran had no official standing beyond being a personal enterprise of Abu-Bekr and Omar; but a few years later this text acquired a great importance when the Caliph Othman set out to establish what was to be the canonical text of the Koran.

After Abu Bekr's death this first recension of Zaid's became Caliph Omar's property, and he left it to his daughter Hafsa, Muhammed's widow. The fact alone would have given it a semi-official status. One must admit that there was a difference between the collected fragments which composed the leaves (Sohof), and the edition of Zaid taken from these leaves. The original leaves had now lost their importance, and became nothing more than souvenirs for Muhammed's widow.

However, this edition of the Koran by Zaid was not the only one. There were others, particularly those attributed to the four companions of Muhammed: Obay ben Kaab, Abdallah ben Masud, Abu-Musa Abdallah al ashari and Miqdad ben Amr.

[1] See page 176.

These editions presented divergencies in detail on which we need not dwell. The important point about these divergencies is that they created divisions among the believers. The first of these editions was adopted by the people of Damascus; the second of those of Kufa, the third by those of Basra, and the fourth by the people of Homs.

Dangerous discussions threatened the unity of Islam. According to tradition it was General Hodaifa who advised the Caliph Othman towards 650, to establish a final edition of the Koran. Othman charged Zaid ben Tsabit, the author of the first edition, as well as other Kureishites to establish it.

It may be permissible to attribute to Othman a political as well as a religious motive in this attempt. Having attained his position with great difficulty he wanted to consolidate his authority by fixing a final text of the Sacred Book, a "ne varietur" text. Of this text several copies were made. One was kept in Medina and considered as the exemplary text. The others were probably sent to Kufa, Basra and Damascus–military centres, or towns whose inhabitants were adherents of one of the divergent versions of the Koran. Othman, the tradition tells us, made one of the copies himself; if so, it must have been the Medina copy. Yet it is more probable that Zaid made it himself on Othman's instructions.

According to tradition, this official Koran contained two chapters less than the Obay edition, and two chapters more than the Ibn-Mas'ud edition. Further, certain differences in the writing and the words also differentiated the copies.

Here a more important question arises: does this version of Othman contain apocryphal passages?

The Kharidjites for example reject the 12th chapter, declaring that the amorous nature of the story of Joseph with the Egyptian woman is incompatible with a sacred book, and that inspiration of this sort from Allah is impossible. But it is only one part of this chapter which deals with the story to which objection is taken. Tradition states that the story was contained in the oldest private editions. Further, Nöldeke remarks judiciously that the style and the language of this chapter are in keeping with the rest of the Koran.

The Shi'ites, on the other hand, affirm that passages referring to Ali and his family were suppressed by Othman's orders. Their argument in favour of this affirmation is the incoherence of certain passages. They believe that the authentic copy is handed over in secret by each Imam to his successor, and that it will be revealed when the hidden Imam makes himself manifest.[1]

It is practically certain that the Koran which has come down to us does not contain the totality of Muhammed's revelations. On the other hand there have been found several explanatory notes, interpolations (not of great consequence) and changes in the order of the sentences. But these do not seem to be falsifications, against which the believers would certainly at once have protested; and the oldest historians are silent on this point. Twenty-seven chapters belong to the period which preceded the Hegira. They began by isolated letters which still embarrass both the Muslem and the non-Muslem exegetists of the Koran. The Muslem scholars, after trying to understand these abbreviations, concluded by considering

[1] See page 187.

them as mysteries only known to Allah. Certain European Orientalists have accepted them as abbreviations; others wished to see in those isolated letters the initials of the names of those who first made copies of the Koran under Zaid. As to the titles of the chapters they were of a later date, and the division into verses also came later.

One must not take it that the edition of the Koran established by Othman's orders underwent no alterations subsequently. The alterations are however due to three causes: the faults committed by the copyists; the survival of the old form of the text which the readers and professional reciters remembered; the insufficiency and lack of precision of the Arabic characters themselves, which make it easy to confound letters with each other; and errors might also creep in where there are no short vowels. Further the Omayyads were not seriously concerned with religious questions, and did not make attempts to prevent divergencies. But with time these divergencies became serious, and disquieting, and led, after research and study, to the establishment of the definite official text in the 10th century. It was based on the authority of seven famous doctors of religion, each being helped by two well-known reciters. This was somewhat arbitrary, but it did not stop discussions. In the 11th century the authority of these was accepted. Of the seven manners of chanting (reciting) the Koran, two have remained in use: one is particular to Egypt, the other to North Africa. On the other hand, in the second half of the 13th century, vocal signs were added: first, dots; and later dashes, which might avoid all error in reading.

CONTENTS AND CHRONOLOGY OF THE

KORAN. The order of the Suras (chapters) is established according to their respective lengths. The shortest (they are also the earliest) are placed at the end of the Koran. Zaid and his companions could not base their classification on the meaning of the verses, because of the fragmentary character of the revelations. Nor could they base it on a chronological order, as it was already too late to be exact. Nevertheless this order, based only on decreasing length of the chapters, has two exceptions: the last two Suras (113 and 114) being those lacking in the edition of Ibn Mas'ud are not the shortest, but they have a special character of their own, for they are in reality only formulas against evil spells. On the other hand, the first Sura (Fatiha, which means, that which opens) contains only seven verses. It was put at the beginning because it is a prayer. After chanting it the chanter always says Amin (amen) which is not done for the other chapters. The Koran even recommends that this chapter be read often.[1]

This artificial order adopted by Zaid and his companions, did not satisfy thoughtful minds. Even in early days commentators noticed striking differences in style in the different parts of the Koran, and they have also remarked furtive allusions to certain events in Muhammed's life. With that the question of the chronology of the Suras was seriously considered.

The chronology had certainly to be based on the causes which occasioned the revelations, but exact information on that subject was scarce. It seems nevertheless, that the 8th Sura was occasioned by the battle of Badr;[2] the 33rd Sura by the War of

1 Chap. 1:v. 1-7.

2 See page 43.

Ditch;[1] and the 48th Sura by the peace of Hudaibiya.[2] In the 30th Sura one finds a mention of the defeat inflicted on the Byzantines by the Persians. But these instances are few, and belong to the Medina period. Muslem commentators have tried to discover in the isolated verses of the Koran allusions to small historical events; but the results obtained have quite often been disputable.

Therefore a direct examination of the style seems preferable to historical evidences. Several Arab commentators have already made tentative studies by this method. Samarqandi noted that the Suras revealed in Medina differed from the Suras revealed in Mecca by the character of the questions addressed to the believers. In the earlier period it is "O men!," in the later it is "O believers!" Using this as the basis of a critical survey of the Koranic text two periods emerge more or less clearly: the period at Mecca before the Hegira, and that at Medina, after the Hegira. This criterion, without being absolute, gives satisfactory results.

A. *BEFORE THE HEGIRA.* Regarding the Suras of the first period, tradition gives us very little information. The chronology of Muhammed's life is uncertain especially for the years immediately before the Hegira. Ibn Isham, the best biographer of Muhammed, gives hardly any dates, therefore it is very difficult to know with any precision the chronology of the Meccan Suras. Nevertheless certain ideas in the Koran belong to this first period: those are, when Muhammed affirms with ardour the resurrection of the dead and the oneness of God; when he

[1] See page 43.
[2] See page 43.

protests vehemently against the accusation of being a poet; when he condemns the pagan custom of burying daughters alive. All these obviously belong to Meccan revelations. There is an important point to note here: Muhammed's dominating idea in the beginning was not so much the proclamation of monotheism, as it was the announcement of the Day of Judgment—probably an idea taken from the Christians.

Basing his study on criteria taken from the Koran, especially its style and vocabulary, the German Orientalist, G. Weil, followed by Nöldeke, established three divisions in the Suras revealed at Mecca.

(a). In the first of these three divisions, the most beautiful in a literary sense, the style is grandiose and coloured with daring imagery. The verses are short and very rhythmical, they contain both simple and strong homilies with somewhat obscure meanings; both as ideas or as allusions they escape us. Further this first group has frequent oaths based generally on natural phenomena,[1] but several of them are enigmatic,—they summon men to think of their salvation. These Suras are short, the sentiments they express are tumultuous, and they were not clearly understood, even by Muhammed's contemporaries. The 96th Sura is considered the oldest among them.

(b). The Suras of the second group are calmer. Oaths give place to the formula: "This is the revelation of Allah!" or "Say!" which is the command of Allah to His Prophet to speak. The annunciation of the Day of Judgment gives place to the proclamation of Monotheism. Muhammed has decidedly broken with idol-worshippers. The Suras become

[1] See page 96.

longer. One finds in them—though still vague enough—rules of conduct and ritual, as well as allusions to prophets who preceded Muhammed.

(c). In the third group, legends concerning prophets multiply, for instance, the confused legends of the Jewish Hagada. These legends comprise about 1500 verses; that is, one-fourth of the Koran. They try to explain to infidels how men of ancient times, having refused to listen to prophets, were struck by God. This third group is full of repetitions, and its style is less firm. It is oratorical rather than poetical and is the least remarkable part of the Koran, and this in spite of the interest of the folk-lore presented in the legends. The oaths so frequent in the older Suras disappear completely. Allah is designated quite often with the word "Rahman," which means merciful. This word disappears in the later Suras which fact is explained by an Orientalist by suggesting that Muhammed was afraid lest the Muslems imagined the "Merciful" to be a different divinity. In the treaty of Hudaibiya, the Meccans rejected the formula containing the word "Rahman," and replaced it by the ancient formula: "In Thy name, O Allah!"

Hence, the first group with its poetic tone, corresponds to the first four years of Muhammed's Mission; the second group, with its half poetic and half oratorical tone, corresponds to the fifth and the sixth years; the third group, with its oratorical tone only, contains the Suras revealed after the sixth year of Muhammed's mission before the Hegira. These are the divisions adopted by Nöldeke for the Meccan revelations of the Koran. Goldziher says: "Scenes painted with ardent colours, dealing with the Day of Judgment, exhortations to men to make them give up their impious and profane life; stories of ancient peoples and their conduct in regard to prophets sent to them; the proof of the absolute power of God in the creation of the world and the admirable development of men, and the dependence of His creatures on Him, whom he can destroy or resurrect—these are the contents of the oldest part of this revealed Book."

B. *AFTER THE HEGIRA*. Prescriptions, that is, specific instructions begin only in the parts revealed after the Hegira. These Suras of the Medina period are the work of a religious and political legislator who having done his preaching had to lay down the principles of conduct for a new society. As to the style of these Suras, it does not differ from that of the third group of Suras of the Meccan period, though new words are introduced in different prescriptions. Opinion differs as to which is the last verse: several authors agree on the 5th verse of the 5th chapter. This part does not lack allusions to the events of the time: respect for the Prophet and his family; praise of those who died in the Way of Allah; attacks against the Hypocrites (the Pharisees of the Muslems); an attack on the idea of the Trinity. "Messiah, Jesus son of Mary, is only an Apostle of Allah, . . . Believe therefore in Allah and His apostles, and say not Three." [1] Jesus appears only in the Suras revealed at Medina. The Medina revelations also contain attacks on the Jews. It is well to remember that in the Meccan revelations Abraham appears only as an old prophet, without any reference to his relation to the Arabs; but in the Medina revelations, that is after Muhammed's break with the Jews, Abraham is attached to the Arabs; not only because

[1] Chap. 4:171.

he had built the Kaaba as a sanctuary together with his son Ishmael; but also as the founder of that pure primitive religion which Muhammed has come to re-establish—the religion of Abraham which the Jews and Christians had deformed.

Civil, penal and religious regulations are mostly found in the 2nd, 4th and 5th Suras, and these comprise about 500 verses and form one tenth of the Koran. Nevertheless, one must not look for a regular code in the Medina Suras. One must affirm once again that contrary to an erroneous idea one often meets, Muslems do not judge everything from the Koran. Nor must one get the idea that the Medina Suras are exclusively of a legislative nature. Some of the verses are among the most beautiful passages in religious writing; certain others summarise with perfect clarity the belief and the duty of the good Muslem. Here is an example: [1]

"Piety consists not in turning your faces to the East or the West. Pious is he who believes in Allah, in the Last Day, in the Angels, in the Book, in the Prophets; and for the love of Allah gives from his possessions to the near kin, to the orphans, to the needy, to the wayfarer, to those who ask; he who gives to liberate captives, observes prayer, pays the poor-rate and fulfills his promises; he who is patient in distress and in affliction and in time of conflict. They are the just and they are those who fear the Lord." [2]

Goldziher finds, justly too, in these Koranic prescriptions a reaction on the one hand against the

1 Chap. 2:128. "Our Lord! make us submissive to Thee, and raise from our offspring a nation submitting to Thee, show us our ways of devotion and turn to us mercifully, surely Thou art the Oft-returning to mercy, the Merciful!"

2 Chap. 2:177.

barbaric complications of pagan ritual, and on the other hand an eclectic character. For example pilgrimage is derived from Arab paganism: [1] the form of Muslem prayer is influenced by Eastern Christianity; the fast seems like the Jewish Fast of Pardon. But there are still other influences. Goldziher sees in them traces of Gnosticism and Parsee-ism, especially in the verses called "the Light." [2]

II. The Sunna

As long as Muhammed lived he governed the Muslem community. But when he died the Muslems saw that the prescriptions of the Koran did not answer all their social needs. From that arose the necessity of adding to the prophetic revelation something which would be able to complete the Koranic prescription whenever the occasion demanded.

At first three procedures were instituted to deal with such exigencies. If the solution of a problem was not found in the Koran, "precedents" taken from Muhammed's acts constituted a guide. This was called the "Sunna." In the second place the ancient customs of Medina were taken as guides, for Muhammed himself had borrowed from them; if these two procedures did not meet the case, then the judge made use of his personal sense of equity. This was called "Ray."

Two contradictory conceptions of the Law existed, therefore side by side from the earliest days of Islam. On the one hand was the utilisation of the legal prescriptions left by Muhammed—a conception based

[1] See page 156.

[2] Chap. 24:v. 35.

on documentary authority; on the other hand was the conception of independent research, a conception of a speculative nature. In the early days of Islam the word "faqih" was used for this. The term is derived from the word "Figh" meaning science of Law. And the word Faqih means jurist. A Faqih (jurist), functioning when there was an insufficiency of legislative prescriptions in the Koran, and, too, no adequate precedents, could make use of his "Ray." But this procedure, which became very important in the course of time, was at first restricted by the Sunna.

What does Sunna mean exactly? In the Koran one comes across such expressions as "Sunna of ancestors," "Allah's Sunna"; the latter being used as "Allah's attitude towards the people of old times who were punished for their unbelief." But outside the Koran the word "Sunna" signifies the facts, gestures, acts and words of Muhammed. Wensinck justly declares, "the observances of Sunna can be in a certain sense used as the imitation of Muhammed." The word "Sunna" can be extended to mean the summary of the customs and conceptions of the oldest Muslem community. On it are based the practice and the theory of the Orthodox Muslem. As in the case of the Jews, it is the super-imposing of the oral tradition on the written one. Those who break away from "Sunna" fall into an innovation (bid'a). With time, the word "bid'a" began to mean "heresy," and became almost synonymous with Kufr (disbelief); though "bid'a" is the result of an error committed while searching for truth. But, while the conservative elements forbade "bid'a" (innovation), the liberal element authorised it in certain cases, as they took into consideration the evolution of Islam based on the "Idjma" (consensus).[1]

It was said among Moslems in early times that "if the Sunna could do without the Koran, the Koran could not do without the Sunna." The term "people of Sunna" (Ahl-as-Sunna) or the Sunnites, which designates the Orthodox Muslems, is derived from this.

The propagators of the "Sunna" were the companions of Muhammed who could remember the words or acts, and even the silences of the Prophet, as expression of his opinion in regard to a given case. Therefore the "Sunna" in a very short time began to complete the word of Allah, either by being in accordance with it, or by explaining it, or by introducing a new element. The study of the "Sunna" created side by side with the jurisconsults (those who interpreted and disputed texts) a class of scholars who collected and fixed all the traditions (Hadith) in regard to the smallest details of the Prophet's life and that of his companions.

III. Traditions (Hadith)

How were these traditions, which are thousands in number, collected?

At first it was the Sahabis, that is the companions of Muhammed, who supplied them; but later it was the Tabi'un, who were the successors of the companions, that is the first generation after Muhammed. Later still it was the successors of the successors who supplied the traditions. A "Hadith" (tradition) is composed of two parts: the text (matn) and preceding the text the names of those who have

1 See page 117.

collected it (Isnad, meaning foundation). Goldziher in his "Dogme" cites textually several of these Hadiths which are among the most beautiful. Here is an example of words ascribed to Muhammed:

"Love the poor; look always to those who are below you, never to those above you; ask nothing from anyone; be faithful to your parents even if they give you pain; tell the truth always even if it is bitter, don't let yourself be discouraged in the Way of Allah even by insults. . . ."

The expansion of Islam brought it in contact with foreign institutions. Their influence over its social evolution obliged the traditionalists gradually to a "pia fraus"; they modernised certain traditions in order to make them answer the needs of the jurisdiction of their time. This led to some flagrant anachronisms which strike the Muslem critics themselves.

The religions of the conquered peoples were not without some influence on the evolution on the "Hadith." Goldziher finds passages from the Christian Apocrypha and reminiscent of Jewish as well as Hellenic ideas that are attributed to Muhammed. Goldziher says: "It is a fascinating problem . . . to determine the sources and the far off ramifications of these divers materials, and to discover the currents of thought which gave them life." Goldziher and Snouck Hurgronje have shown that several among the Hadith were reflections of ideas which dominated early Islam and this naturally confers on them great value in regard to the evolution of Islam. Some of the Hadith reflect political tendencies, by being favourable sometimes to the partisans of Othman, and sometimes to Ali-ites, and this in itself indicates the epoch in which they were established.

Muslem scholars began at an early date to study critically the texts of the Hadith as well as that of the Koran; especially the agents who have transmitted the Hadith texts. In the numerous biographies of persons who have collected the Hadith one reads about the degree of their reliability, and the degree is quite often a subject of controversy. All this led to a classification of the Hadith, a complicated enough classification in regard to the degree of reliability of the collectors. For instance the "Taqrib" written by Nawawi (translated by Marçais) which is a good example.

Collections of Hadith are numerous. At first they were arranged according to their authors (Isnad: the word Mosnad is given to this form of collection). But later, the Hadith were arranged according to the material they contained, and divided into chapters. This manner of classification of the Hadith took the name of "Masannaf," meaning divided into categories. Six collections of this second kind were made in the 9th century by scholars of Persian origin. The authority of this collection is recognised as second only to that of the Koran. It must be added that the part the Persians played in the science of Islamic theology is considerable, as was recognised by the great Arab historian, Ibn-Khaldun, in these terms:

"It is a remarkable fact that the greater number of scholars who have distinguished themselves among Muslems by their ability in science are of alien origin. The examples to the contrary are rare. . . . Similarly those persons who knew the traditions (Hadith) by heart were of Persian origin.[1] All the great scholars who have written about the fundamental principles of jurisprudence, all those who have distinguished themselves in dogmatic theology, and the greater number of those who have specialised in the interpretation of the Koran, were Persians . . . the teaching of all science has become a special art of the Persians."

At this period, the Muslem doctors of law had reached a certain amount of unanimity, due to the political unity of Islam being firmly established. The authors of these collections were not the innovators they are sometimes thought to be; but to them falls the merit of having collected all the Hadith which were then considered as authentic. The authority of these collections however was generally recognised only some time after. Eventually extracts and commentaries on these collections were made. For, the Hadith were often written in very archaic language and needed explanation. All that became subject matter for the universities and the colleges of the Islamic world.

IV. The Science of Law
(Fiqh: Juris prudentia)

In the meantime, while the traditionalists attached themselves exclusively to the letter, other scholars began to discuss the spirit of the law. To the "Ilm," which represented the traditional theology and the canonical law, was added the "Fiqh" which comprised ethical speculation. The relations of

[1] Recent researches prove that quite a number of these scholars mentioned as Persian were of Turkish origin.

Arabs with people much more subtle than themselves, such as the Persians and the Syrians, and the development of a taste for luxury accelerated by their conquests made the legislative basis of the growing Muslem society inadequate. The Omayyads, ruling in Damascus, began like the kings of ancient Arabia to scandalise the pietists who were then living in Medina and who kept a strict observance of the law as far as they could. The result was a scission between the spiritual and temporal power, and this state of affairs did not make it easy to adapt jurisprudence to practical life.

But when the Abassides came into power a change took place, at least to all appearances. The Omayyads were primarily temporal rulers; while the Abassides were both temporal and spiritual. In contrast with their predecessors they patronised and conciliated the clerical party whose authority they needed in order to establish their legitimacy. The union of religion and the state—a Persian idea—was realised in their time.

With the Abasside advent to power, the sacred texts grew in importance, for they were studied not merely from a sense of piety, but for their application to practical life. Jurisprudence was to be organised, but in strict accordance with the divine law. The conquests also favoured the development of jurisprudence, for they brought the Arabs into contact with peoples who were ruled by ancient laws, such as the Jewish, Roman and Persian; and these laws are not without some influence on the elaboration of the Muslem law itself. As a matter of fact, this jurisprudence was not spontaneous among the Arabs, but was organised in the 11th century in Syria and Iraq owing to contact with the Christian schools of law. Goldziher has noted several equivalent technical terms among the Arabs and the Latins, of which we will speak later.

Very soon however, contradictory tendencies arose among the jurists: one party insisted on basing law on the Hadith, while the other, noticing uncertainties and contradictions among the numerous Hadith, looked for some other basis for their judicial authority. Hence there came into existence schools of jurisprudence which differed both in method and in interpretation.

The oldest attempt at codification from the Sunnite (orthodox) point of view, is the collection of Hadith, entitled Mawatta (the level path), which was made by Malik ibn Anas, who died in 795. This work is a compromise between a collection of Hadith and jurisprudence proper. It proceeds from the text (matn) of the Hadith, without any regard to the agents by whom the Hadith were transmitted (Isnad). Malik proposed to construct a judicial system founded directly on Hadith. His work represents the judicial conceptions of the scholars of Medina in the 8th century. Malik's principal source is naturally the Koran, and then the Sunna of Muhammed and his companions, but he occasionally adds something from the customs and laws of Medina. Further, he admits that the traditions, though necessary as a basis, may be modified if they are found to be in opposition to the public good (the principle of Istislah). He also invokes another principle for use whenever there is a need; the consensus (Idjma: consensus doctorum ecclesiae) of the doctors of law of Medina on a given question. In brief, Malik maintains tradition, but accepts personal interpretation (ray: opinio prudentium) in so far as it is necessary for the public good. Goldziher points out an analogy between this method and the "corrigere jus propter utilitatem publicam" of Roman law.

About the same time, other systems of jurisdiction were being elaborated in Syria by Awzai, who died in 774. They achieved great success, particularly in Iraq, which was an intellectual centre. The most eminent representative of this school was Abu-Hanifa, who died in 767, and who propagated the ideas of the school more by personal teaching than by his writings. He was of Persian origin and probably did not, like Malik who was judge by profession, get a chance to put his theories into practice. He was more of a speculative jurist. Three principles characterise his system: Preponderance of "ray" (personal reasoning based on common sense); "Qiyas" (principle of analogy, "analogia") corrected by the procedure of "Istihsan." The "Istihsan" corresponds to the "Istislah" of Malik, and may be paraphrased thus: From a given text in a certain case analogy indicates this course of action, but circumstances make it preferable (Istihsan) to act in that manner.

Abu-Hanifa's doctrine was first propagated by his pupils throughout the Orient, and was supported by the Seljukid Sultans,[1] and later by the Ottoman Sultans. That of Malik was propagated in the West, particularly in North Africa.

However, the two systems, that of Malik and that of Abu-Hanifa, are not so different from each other as is commonly supposed, except that the former is more moderate in the use of "ray" (personal opinion). The

[1] See page 227.

greatest difference between these two systems is with regard to consensus (Idjma). The Malikite consensus is restricted to the doctors of law of Medina, and therefore remains strictly local; but this restricted consensus was to be extended quite soon by the leader of a new school of jurisprudence: Shafi'i, who died in 820.

As a matter of fact, while Malik used the consensus (Idjma) as an incidental principle, Shafi'i established it as a general principle; and the general Idjama of doctors of law, thus established by Shafi'i, delegated infallibility to the community—he made the community virtually the only ultimate legislative power in Islam. Henceforward doctors of Law in Islam could do as they wished, provided they were unanimously agreed.

It is evident that this "Idjma" could not exist in actuality as a general agreement of the doctors of law of all times. In the first place, how could it be obtained? Islam had no Councils and Synods; in fact the only time when there was a congress of Muslems was in the 20th century with regard to the future of the Caliphate. The consensus of Malik was strictly confined to the consensus of the doctors of Medina; and the Wahhabites[1] imitated the Zahirites, and made it still more restricted. They reduced the "Idjma" to the companions of the Prophet. As for the Shafi'ites, they restricted themselves to defining the "Idjma" as the unanimous agreement between the doctors of law of a given time. Goldziher says: "If any universally tolerated and recognised usage lasts for a long time it becomes a "Sunna" in itself. For several generations, pious theologians have com-

[1] See page 252.

plained against bid'a (innovation); but a lapse of time and the consensus (Idjma) of opinion did not only tolerate it but fixed it, after which to consider it as innovation becomes a transgression." It was this "Idjma" which consecrated the final text of the Koran; the six collections of "Hadiths"; the holy days, and the anniversary of the birth of the Prophet; the belief in miracles, the existence and the power of intercession, and the cult of saints. The celebration of the birth of the Prophet (mawlid-an-nabi) was added to the religious holidays, and after the 8th century it was no longer considered as a "bid'a" (innovation) but a "Sunna." It is celebrated throughout the entire Muslem world in the month of Rabi-ul-avval.

Gaudefroy-Demombynes says: The term "Idjma" (consensus) is very vague, and its interpretation has varied a great deal. It is not a consistent term with an absolutely defined meaning, but is understood to be a latent truth concerning the Koran and the Sunna, which must necessarily express the Divine Will. The date at which the Muslem savants arrived at an agreement is not stated, nor is there any official confirmation of it, and no one promulgated it. It is a matter of opinion and nothing else. What strikes one most about this doctrine, which was established after long and passionate discussions, is the absence of general principles."

Shafi'i, by attributing so much importance to the consensus, was logically led to reject "ray" (personal opinion), that is the "Istihsan" of the Hanifite and the "Istislah" of the Malikite. He retained "Qiyas," that is, judgment by analogy, and declared in his Risala, (the exposition of his doctrine) that it was permitted to use "Qiyas" "in cases which are not treated in the Koran, the Sunna or the Idjma." By this he greatly reduced the applicability of "Qiyas."

According to Shafi'i, the authoritative basis of Islamic jurisprudence (Ususl-al-Fiqh) are the following, arranged in the order of their importance: Koran, "Sunna," "Idjma" and "Qiyas." Snouck Hurgronje, in his exposition of these four principles, characterises them perfectly; the former two are the historical basis of the law; "Idjma" (which contains the two former) is the dogmatic basis without which nothing is solid; and "Qiyas" is the logical basis.

The Shafi'ite doctrine in spite of, or because of, its eclecticism, did not gain a general acceptance. Bokhari, the great traditionalist, though a Shafi'ite himself, inserted in his collection of "Hadiths" a chapter containing traditions which were reprobations of "ray" and "Qiyas"; analogous traditions are found in Darimi's collection. Further, from Shafi'i's time onward, a reaction by the partisans of Hanbalite and Zahirite jurisprudence set in.

The Hanbalite school has derived its name from its founder, Ahmad ibn Hanbal who died in 855, and was an old pupil of Shafi'i. Strictly speaking, Ibn Hanbal did not establish a system. He pronounced on a certain number of questions on jurisdiction in the course of his teaching, and these pronouncements were propagated by his pupils. According to Ibn Hanbal, law can only be taken from traditional sources, and this led him to admit traditions (Hadith) of questionable value. He was an enemy in principle of all bid'a, which led to ferocious orthodoxy and provoked bloody conflicts. The Wahhabite movement of the 18th century was derived indirectly from Hanbalism, and is still hostile to innovation. Goldziher says: "The orthodox schools are hostile to bid'a, and only differ in the degree of their hostility." The "Madhab" (system) of the Hanbalites and that of the Hanifites represent in this the two extremes.

Ibn Hanbal admitted "ray" (personal opinion) in a case of absolute necessity. But the Zahirite school, founded by Daudaz-Zahiri in the 9th century, rejected it, and so restricted the consensus only to companions of the Prophet. In other words, Zahirites accept as sources of jurisdiction only the Koran and the Sunna; and the Sunna must be interpreted literally (Zahir: the apparent or literal sense). Though Zahirism found in Ibn Hazm a champion of rare talents in the 11th century, it was unable to maintain a lasting hold on the practice of the law.

Other schools also had an ephemeral existence, such as the school of Awzai (8th century) which rallied for a time the Muslems of Maghreb and Spain to its doctrines; the school of Tabari, founded by the famous theologian and historian, Tabari; the Djaririya school, derived from the Shafi'ism of the 9th and 10th centuries; and the school of Sofyan-at-Thawri, a partisan of the Hadith in the 8th century.

As a matter of fact, jurisprudence had reached its zenith with Shafi'i and the three other schools, which were contemporary, dominated the orthodox Muslems. These schools are called in Arabic "Madhab" [1] which is ordinarily translated as "rite or system," and

[1] Primitive meaning of "Madhab" was "way, passage." In this sense, it means "method," approaching the Greek "methodos." In a less precise but general way it means system. To translate it as "sect" is a grave error. See page 174.

which implies an interpretation from religious sources.

Orthodox Islam has in various times and places adopted one or other of these four systems of jurisprudence; the causes of the preference have been principally from royal support, popular inclination, trade reasons, ease of communication, etc., etc.:

(1). Hanifite Rite: This was accepted by the majority of the Orthodox Muslems because of its liberalism and where there was Ottoman preponderance. Turkey, continental India and China are Hanifite. It has adherents in Egypt and in the Malay Archipelago.

(2). Shafi'ite Rite: In number of adherents it comes second to the Hanifite Rite. Lower Egypt, Hedjaz, South Arabia, eastern Africa and South Africa, Palestine and particularly the Indian Archipelago are its centres.

(3). Malikite Rite: This dominated Spain in the old Muslem days. At the moment, its centres are North Africa, Upper Egypt, western Africa and the Soudan.

(4). Hanbalite Rite: This rite was accepted only in the 12th century and had spread in Syria and Mesopotamia where the Seljukids were propagating Hanifism. In the 14th century it spread once more to Syria, owing to Ibn Taymiya and his disciples. At present it is restricted to Nedjd in Arabia.

Orthodox Islam attributes an equal value to all these four systems. The divergencies are of a secondary nature (Ikhtilaf-al-Madhahib), are only in the domain of the application of the law (Fraou'-al-Fiqh) and not in the principle of the law (usul-al-Fiqh). These differences are mentioned and approved in a

"Hadith." An Orthodox Muslem can freely adopt or change any one rite. At the famous University of al-Azhar of Cairo, each of these four systems is represented by different masters and students. It happens that Hanbalism which was not represented for some years, in 1906 became represented by three professors and twenty-eight students, out of 312 professors and 9069 students. One can summarise the tendencies of these systems by saying that the Malikites and Hanbalites attach a greater importance to the letter of the law, while the Hanifites and the Shafi'ites attach greater importance to the spirit of the law.

The founders of these four orthodox systems of jurisprudence in Islam are all considered as "Mudjtahid mutlak." That is, each of these four doctors is credited with an absolute capacity for formulating a personal opinion on the application of the Koran, the Sunna and the "Qiyas" (principle of analogy) to the procedures of the law particular to their system. These doctors established the fundamental principles of the system of the Islamic law. Jurists who succeeded them were only Mudjtehids and not absolute; that is they could only formulate personal opinion on the application of the law in relation to and within the frame of their particular school. The jurists of the later period were no longer even Mudjtehids. They could only pronounce by a judicial consultation based on one or more precedents (Fatwa: responsa prudentium). These men were called "Mufti," that is those who give the "Fatwa." They could never pronounce on personal opinion, but must always base their pronouncement on a precedent. Nevertheless, several among the later jurists, notably Ibn Taymiya and Soyuti pretended to have the right to "Idjtihad," that is, to a personal opinion. But in general the jurisconsults based their pronouncements on a small number of works on jurisdiction: manuals of "fiqh" with commentaries and glossary, and collections of "fatwas." In Algeria, for example, the Mawatta, the work of Malik, was the basis of the Malikite rite; but it was abandoned in favour of a later work, the Mukhtasar, by Sidi Khalil. Though the latter is called the "abridged," it is more detailed and more complete than the Mawatta. In brief, there is no formal code in Islam in the sense understood by Europeans.

Hence, "fiqh," according to Lammens is defined as: "the ensemble of obligations which the Koranic law (Sharia) imposes on the Muslem in his triple quality of believer, man and citizen of a theocracy." In Muslem law, questions of ritual combine with the questions of civil, criminal and constitutional law. The ritual has been elaborated and developed in the course of centuries, and is not a reflection of the social needs of the present time. It is a theoretic system and some of its prescriptions are mere subtleties resulting from casuistry, and have become less and less applicable. Snouck Hurgronje says:

"From the middle of the first century of the Hegira, the law has become canonical; that is to say, a law conceived and organised with regard to a given state of things . . . a state which existed only under the first four caliphs. Nevertheless it had a vital influence on the ulterior development of Islam. To elaborate laws with regard to the complications of real life is quite different from elaborating a law with regard to an ideal state. This law, nevertheless, has a great pedagogical value for the Muslem world. As a subject of teaching, it has remained the faithful depository of a religious ideal which protests against reality."

On the other hand, Goldziher also judiciously notes that the speculative character of Muslem jurisdiction has affected the religious life itself, as well as the actual feeling for the Divine.

Meanwhile, a study of the historical evidence leads one to the conclusion that practice soon led Muslems to drop some of the exigencies of this ideal "fiqh" and several parts of it became obsolete. Further, the intervention of the sovereign substituted a local law for the "fiqh." Finally the custom law (orf, ada, particularly among Berbers and then known as "qanun") had often the same prestige as before Islam. This brought about at times an absolute separation of spiritual from temporal jurisdiction, in such cases as did not strictly depend on the religious law. In Morocco, for example, printed copies of the "Custom Law of Faz" are regularly consulted, and made use of by the Cadis. As there has never been an official legislative body in Islam to fix the laws, the law evolved of itself. The consequence was a superimposition of a civil justice on the Shari'a, which remained in force in questions of ritual. For example, the commercial law followed practical solutions rather than theory. On the other hand, constitutional and penal laws, as well as taxation and property rights passed insensibly to the domain of temporal jurisdiction. Religious law had its revenge at the advent of the Ottoman Sultans in Turkey, when they created the office of the Sheik-ul-Islam (Mufti of Constantinople). But in modern times social changes obliged the Turkish Government to attempt a codification of the civil law, and that long before the Angora Reforms. The Kanum-name, that is, the collection of laws promulgated by the Turkish Ottoman Sultans, belongs to this category. Muhammed II, the Conqueror, issued laws in the middle of the 15th century which regulated the protocols in ceremonials, revenues obtained from the taxes on employments and fines in cases of delinquency. Soliman, in the early 16th century, reorganised the régime of military fiefs already established by Murad I, codified farming system in Egypt, fixed the rights and duties of non-Muslem subjects called Riaya,[1] and established police regulations by a series of laws incorporated in his Kanum-name. In 1839, the royal edict Gulkhan (Khatt-Sherif) inaugurated the Tanzimat reforms, which eventually led to the proclamation of a Constitution for the Ottoman Empire in 1876.[2] The revolution of 1906 in Persia led to the proclamation of a Constitution for that country which was completed in 1907.

In other Muslem countries subject to European rule the question of jurisdiction inevitably arose. In the Malay Archipelago (where Islam had penetrated by the end of the 13th century through the intermediary of Arab merchants and sailors) the Dutch retained the old jurisdiction; but their legal specialists have studied with care the local jurisprudence. The

1 Riaya were the non-Muslem subjects who were mostly merchants, artisans and agriculturists and who could not have a military or civil employment. Riaya literally means flock, but this term was judged injurious and changed into "teba" in 1856, which means "subjects."

2 The Constitution accorded to the Ottoman Empire in 1876 was suppressed by Abdul-Hamid. It was re-established after the constitutional revolution of 1908.

British in India and the French in Algeria[1] have undertaken to codify the Muslem law.

In Algeria the question regarding codification of the Muslem law concerns only certain parts of it. The most delicate points which have not yet been adapted are: the personal statutes; the marriage laws; the respective duties and rights of the different members of the family; successions and statutes dealing with real estate and habeas corpus.[2] Alfred Bell, in an article in the Rev. His. Religions (1927), summarises the work accomplished on this codification, and enumerates the possible advantages and the disadvantages of its official application.

[1] Algerians are the adherents of the Malikite "Madhab." Hanifism and Malikism struggled for supremacy for centuries in North Africa. The two rites had expanded side by side in the 9th century. From the 10th century onward (see page 30), when the Fatimids ruled, Hanifism alone could hold its own against Shi'ism. But in the 11th century when the Zirids overthrew the suzerainty of the Fatimids (see page 31) the Malik gained on Hanifism, and in spite of the Turkish support of Hanifism in the 16th century, Hanifism remained as the rite of the minority. Tripolitans are also Malikites, which has obliged the Italians to study the collection of Sidi-Khalil (translated a long time before into French).

[2] See page 154.

CHAPTER IV

Dogma and Law

I. Dogma

Two koranic verses enumerate the fundamental dogmatic tenets of Islam: "O believers, believe in Allah, in His Apostle and the Book which He has revealed to His Apostle, and the writings which He had revealed before. Whosoever disbelieves in Allah, His Apostle and His angels and His Apostles and the Last Day, errs completely."[1] Another verse[2] enunciates the same more briefly.

These are the fundamental articles of faith. But the Muslem must have two other things in addition to faith. Faith (Iman) must be accompanied by virtue (Ihsan) and by submission to the Will of Allah (Islam). In the Koran, Islam (submission to the Will of Allah and the sentiment of dependence) and Ihsan (virtue) are at times used synonymously; and at other times they are given distinct meanings. In the 49th chapter and the 14th verse, it says to the dwellers of the desert: ". . . You do not have Iman (faith); say rather that you have Islam (submission to the Will of Allah). Iman has not yet entered your heart."

[1] Chap. 4: 136. One part of this verse has been the subject of great discussion in Islam. "We made no difference between any of His Apostles," which means that Muhammed is no greater than the prophets before him.

[2] Chap. 2:285.

The exact significance of "Iman," that is, faith, was for a long time a subject of discussion among the theologians, and finally Orthodox opinion declared faith (Iman) to be composed of three elements: Tasdiq, Iqrar and Amal; meaning inner acceptation of belief, confession by word of mouth, and action (good conduct and works).

These dogmas were not officially issued in Islam, as was the case with other religions; for example, the Credo of Christianity. Nevertheless, the doctors from the 11th century onward tried to expound briefly the substance of the foundations of the Muslem faith. This kind of writing received the name of Aqida.[1]

The believer who accepts openly these three elements of faith is among the elect. Any one who confesses to the first two elements (Tasdiq and Iqrar) without practising the third (acts), dies in mortal sin, if he does not repent, and will be chastised. Nevertheless, Orthodox Muslem opinion interprets fire as purgatory, rather than Hell; and believes that such a man can be cleansed by fire, and eventually enter Heaven. This point was also discussed by the other schools. As to one who professes and practises without inner belief, he is a hypocrite (Monafiq), and an infidel.

Can faith increase and decrease? The Koran speaks at times of an increase in faith.[2] But the problem is not solved. There are those who consider faith to be essentially an inner acceptance (Tasdiq) and therefore they exclude variation; there are others who consider faith (Iman) not only a matter of inner accep-

1 See Carra de Vaux's article in the Encyclopedia of Islam.

2 Chap. 3:2; Chap. 9:124.

tance but also a manner of action (Amal); therefore it can become stronger or weaker.

BELIEF IN ALLAH. The first article of faith as well as its essential dogma, is belief in One God. It is expressed in this formula: "La ilâh illâllah," meaning "There is no god but God." To Tewhid (belief in One God) is opposed "Shirk" (polytheism), and its adherents are called Mushrikin, that is, "those who believe in more than one god." They are attacked in the more recent parts of the Koran, and considered to be on the same plane as infidels (Kafir). In the works of jurisprudence, the word Mushrik is as often used as the word Kafir to designate the unbeliever. Nevertheless on the subject of Kafir, theologians have established several degrees of unbelief (Kufr).

We have already seen what Allah meant to the pagan Arab. What does Allah mean to Islam? Allah is not only one God like the Hebraic Jehovah, but also resembles Jehovah in his vindictiveness and jealousy. (He must not be confused with the Elohim, for He is unique.) In different parts of the Koran occur various epithets to describe the nature of Allah, such as: the First, the Last, the Apparent, the Invisible, etc. Pious Muslems have taken the most beautiful of these epithets and have used them in their litany. These are about a hundred, including the name Allah itself. Macdonald says: "From all these epithets there emerges the idea of a Being which suffices unto itself, all powerful, omniscient, and containing all things in itself, an eternal and unique reality." Naturally theologians have discussed at infinite length the nature of Allah.

At a later date, the study of these names led the Muslem theologians—probably under the influence of Christian doctors—to define attributes (sifat) hidden behind these names. Orthodox Islam finally declared that "the attributes of Allah were eternal." "His attributes are neither Allah himself nor are they other than he." (La houa wa la Ghairuhu). We will see the opinion of the Mutazelites on the point later.[1]

This supreme Being who suffices unto itself, has nevertheless created the world. Hence the name found in the Koran: Al-Khaliq (the Creator). How did this creation (khalq) take place? In the Koran the creation of man dominates the rest. Everything is created for man. The world was created in six days. But while Allah made the world out of absolute nothingness, he made man out of matter.[2] Allah formed man in His own image, and breathed His spirit into him. This creation is a sign of the power and the goodness of Allah. But He has created it only for a predetermined period,[3] and it remains purposely imperfect. Men are unstable,[4] men are covetous,[5] they are weak, inconsiderate and, above all, ungrateful.[6] Though Allah has made all people as one, they have quarrelled among themselves, and have become divided because of their jealousy.[7]

What is the formation of the physical world? According to tradition, there is a circular mountain around the world called Kaf (probably of Iranian origin). The space between the world and this mountain is not surmountable. According to other

[1] See page 205.
[2] Chap. 22:v. 5.
[3] Chap. 46:v. 3.
[4] Chap. 22:v. 11.
[5] Chap. 70:v. 21.
[6] Chap. 17:v. 69.
[7] Chap. 2:v. 204.

traditions, the earth is presented as resting on the shoulders of an angel (analogous to the giant Atlas), who leans against a rock; the rock is in turn resting on a bull, and the bull is standing on a swimming fish. This is undoubtedly borrowed from the Hindu and Hebraic cosmogonies. When the earth was created, Allah established Himself in the heavens, which were nothing but smoke; and He then divided the heavens into seven parts, each having a special function.[1]

ANGELS AND DEMONS. The substance out of which the angels are made is light, and they have no sex. They obey Allah passively. The four Hebraic archangels have been adopted by Islam as the "Muqarribin" (those near Allah); they are as gigantic as the "Kerubim." Djabrail carries the divine orders, Israfil is ready to blow the trumpet on the Day of Judgment, and Azrail is the archangel of death. Every man has two guardian angels who write down his good and bad actions. This is sometimes done by two other angels called Katibain, meaning the two scribes. These guardian angels do their work at dawn or in the evening, the moments favourable to temptation.

Munkir and Nakir are the angels of the grave; Ridwan is the angel who guards Heaven, and Malik the angel who guards Hell. There are other angels who support the divine throne.

The angels were created before Adam. When Adam appeared, Allah ordered the angels to worship him and all obeyed except Iblis (corruption of the Greek diabolos), or the devil (Shaytan, Satan, borrowed from Judaism), who refused because he was

[1] Chap. 41:v. 10-12.

created out of fire, and would not stoop to adore one who was created out of dust. Allah cursed him, but gave him a respite until the Day of Judgment. Meanwhile Satan profits by this respite to lead human beings astray having begun with Adam and Eve. At the end of time, he will be thrown, with the other demons who obey him, into Hell. These demons are called by different names, the best known being Djinn (probably from the Latin Genius). The Djinns (which are reminiscent of the Iranian Div) are made of mist or flame, without smoke; and they take divers forms. Their relation to Iblis is not very definite, and it is not certain whether all of them will be condemned. In the pre-Islamic Arabia, these Djinns played the part of nymphs and satyrs. But even in Muhammed's lifetime, pagans recognised them as divinity and sacrifices were made to them. Islam has given them formal recognition, and this has been taken so seriously that there has been discussion as to whether a human being can marry or possess property in common with one of them. Naturally this was exploited mostly by folklore writers and hagiographers.[1]

In the Orient, as well as the Occident, popular belief attributes a certain number of misdeeds to these demons. Just as in the Christian Middle Ages, the Mejnun (possessed) were exorcised, so there were formulas, amulets and talismans which were used to drive away or to appease these powers of darkness who were specially dangerous for women in travail and new-born babes. The Berbers, especially, con-

1 The last three of the Jewish divisions of the Old Testament comprise the books of Psalms, Proverbs, Job, Daniel, Ezra, Nehemiah, Ruth, Esther, Chronicles, Canticles, Lamentations, Ecclesiastes. Students of these are called hagiographers.

sult them for future events. Sometimes the soul of these demons enters the body of a harmful animal. The reluctance of the masses to kill lice is due to this.

Demons are not merely consigned to the earth and to the lower heavens. They take the risk of approaching the borders of the seventh heaven, from whence the angels drive them away by throwing stones which are shooting stars.

Apart from demons, the Koran mentions two other fallen angels: Harut and Marut.[1] These angels are something like the ones mentioned in Genesis, chapter V. They seem to be descended indirectly from the marriage of fallen angels with the daughters of men.

THE PROPHETS. The two articles of faith regarding belief in the revealed books and in the prophets can be reduced to one. The prophets are superior to angels, as the latter did not have to struggle against temptations, and against their own nature. They are the messengers of Allah, sent to reveal religion to man, or to remind them of their sins. Their actual number is in dispute, but one can count them in thousands. "Surely We have sent an Apostle to every nation." But the revealed books were given to men through only a hundred among them. The six principal ones are: Adam, Nuh (Noah), Ibrahim (Abraham), Musa (Moses), Isa (Jesus) and Muhammed who is the last (the seal of prophets). David, Jacob, Joseph and Job are of secondary importance.

Prophets had the gift of performing miracles, but Muhammed himself admits only one miracle; and

[1] Chap. 2:v. 102.

that is the revelation of the Koran. Nevertheless, tradition attributes to him several miracles, one of them being the division of the moon into two. It is mentioned in the Koran as a sign of the Day of Judgment; but commentators have tried to make it appear as an intervention of Muhammed.

Strictly Orthodox opinion in Islam regards the prophets only as saints. Nevertheless, another conception of sainthood also developed at a later date in Islam, of which we will speak later.[1]

THE DAY OF JUDGMENT. The Koran in its oldest parts is full of allusions to the Last Day, and gives astounding descriptions of the events which will announce that Day. For that reason men must repent at once. This idea of resurrection, called Qiyama in Arabic, meaning "the rising," is not so new and absolute as it seems at first. The pagan Arabs believed the dead to continue their life in lesser degree in their graves. Islam adopted this belief. The judgment by the two angels of the grave after death, makes the tomb a preliminary Paradise or Hell, according to Macdonald's interpretation. In the Koran itself, the Day of Judgment applies to persons as individuals and not as masses; and this idea is due to Christian influence, according to Wellhousen's interpretation.

The Koran itself alludes to a limited number of signs, which shall indicate the coming of the Last Day. These passages were studied, and very largely developed. Theologians took a sober attitude on this conception of the Last Day, while the traditionalists and authors of edifications accumulated details. This is specially true of Maqdisi, the Book of Crea-

[1] See page 208.

tion, translated by Huart, which deals with this in its second chapter. Ibn Khaldun's Prolegomena, translated by Slane, also deals with it in its second part.

Before dealing with these signs, it would be well to remember that the Day of Judgment is not considered as being universal. As an example, we can refer to certain traditions which tell us that thousands of believers will enter Heaven without having to give any account of their deeds. To these belong the fighters in the Holy War, who are considered as martyrs.[1]

The first sign of the end of time will be seen in an increase of impiety among men. The temple at Mecca will disappear, and men will forget the Koran. Then a man inspired by Allah will appear upon earth: the Mahdi (meaning the Guided One), who is the Muslem Messiah, and for a time He will establish again Justice and Faith on the earth. But in reality the conception of the advent of Mahdi, which was exploited by Shi'ism, does not come about as easily as is supposed, according to Orthodox opinion in Islam. The traditionalists do speak of it as an ultimate and supreme justice, carried out by one person; but they do not use the word Mahdi, and they do not count the event as a sign of the Day of Judgment. In brief, the idea of Mahdi came into existence in Islam at a later date; and all the Orthodox Muslems do not accept it.

One perceives a certain uncertainty with regard to

1 According to Masse it is only a few authors who have added the fighters of the Holy War to the list of those who will enter Heaven without giving any account of their deeds. The general belief in Islam is that all those who pray, fast, pay the poor-rate and make the pilgrimage enter Heaven.

the Mahdi as Restorer. For the idea of Jesus is superimposed on it, reflecting the apocryphal texts of the Christians. At the end of time there will appear an Antichrist (Dadjdjal), on the subject of which different authors give contradictory details. He will come from a far-off island at a moment when Gog and Magog (savage peoples of Asia) break through the walls which imprison them.[1] The Dadjdjal will be a giant riding an enormous donkey; and his rule will last forty days, during which time he will devastate the world. It is then that Jesus will descend to earth from the sky, and will kill the Antichrist with a stroke of his spear, and then go to Jerusalem to pray. And for forty years, that is until Jesus dies, love and happiness will reign in the world "sheep and wolves will be seen together; children will play with serpents."

Other signs, invented later, which shall point to the destruction of the universe, are given in the Book of Creation.[2] At the first blast of the trumpet by Israfil, nature will be thrown into convulsions, and human beings will try to escape in panic. On the second blast of the trumpet, all human beings will expire. This universal death will be followed by an interval, which will last for a period of forty years. At the end of that period torrential rains will precede the third blast from the trumpet, which will summon all creatures to a general resurrection and an assembly in Jerusalem for judgment. Creatures will stand naked in the presence of Allah, scorched by a hot sun, streaming with perspiration, and each holding

[1] Chap. 18:94.

[2] Part II, page 145. "The Book of Creation," by Magdisi. Trans. by Huart.

the book containing the account of his deeds. Allah will question them one after another, and will weigh their deeds, after which they will have to cross the bridge called "Sirat"—the bridge which spans Hell and leads to Heaven. It is as thin as a hair and as sharp as a sword. It is then that Muhammed will intercede in favour of sinners. Thanks to this intercession, the only sinners who will remain in Hell are those who believe in more than One God. "Everything else He will forgive in whomsoever He wishes." [1]

The exegetists divide the Muslem Hell into seven regions in the manner of the Greek, Assyrian or Christian Hell of the Middle Ages. In the Koran, Hell is designated sometimes as "Nar" meaning fire; and sometimes by the word Djahannam (the Gehenna of the Hebrew: Ge-hinnom). This Djahannam appears as mobile, and certain exegetists, especially Ghazali, imagined it as a kind of monster, very much as in the Mystery plays of Occidental Christianity. In the last stage of this hell is the tree of Zakkum, the flowers of which are heads of demons; there are also a cauldron filled with scalding pitch, and a bottomless pit. The Koran itself hardly mentions any of the infernal tortures which these later Muslem authors have stressed. These are derived from Jewish legends.

Between Hell and Heaven there is an undetermined space, a no man's land, which is called Araf, and is the title given to the 7th chapter of the Koran. Some believe it to be Purgatory, others consider it to be a place where certain souls await Judgment, also

[1] Koran, Chap. 4:v. 116.

called Limbus. The inhabitants of Araf will cry out to the dwellers in Paradise: ". . . Peace be on you . . ." and when their eyes shall turn towards the inmates of the Fire, they shall say: "O Lord, place us not with the unjust." [1]

As for Paradise, called Djanna, meaning the Garden, it is, according to tradition, also divided into several parts. One is called Firdaws, borrowed from the Persian, and corresponding to the Greek word "paradeisos." It is useless to insist on its voluptuous and profane character, such as is described in chapter 37:v. 40-49. In the delights described, the Muslem theologians have seen allegories which have nothing in common with the substance of terrestrial objects. The Houris (Hours), the virgins with black eyes who live with the dwellers of Paradise and remain virgins, are of a different substance from the daughters of men. The Koran presents them as exempt from all corporeal impurity and moral imperfection; but there is no detailed descriptions of them, such as the latest authors have added. Some see in the Houris a trace of Mazdaism. Carra de Vaux supposes them to have been suggested by the Christian mosaics and pictures representing angels.

In addition to these creatures, there are comfortable places to sit and enjoy the pleasures of the palate. Further, there are also cold waters and rivers of milk, wine and honey (salsabil, Zandjabil, Kawthar), reminiscent of the Jewish and Christian Paradise, imagined for the purpose of charming the inhabitants of countries where water is scarce.

The division of Heaven into seven circles compared

[1] Chap. 7:v. 46-47.

with the seven regions of Hell comes later. Over the highest circle grows a Lotus which bounds it, as well as provides shade. This closed Paradise contains the original copy of the Koran and other books as well as certain objects which will be used on the Day of Judgment. These seven heavens are upon seas which expand beyond the skies. Above Paradise is the throne of Allah.

Snouck Hurgronje says: "The doctrine of resurrection and the Day of Judgment when entire humanity will appear before Allah with a background of Heaven and Hell is Muhammed's centre of faith. It was this doctrine which he opposed formally to the ideas of the Arab world to which he was to bring Allah's message. The pre-Islamic Arab mind was only concerned with the life on earth, ignoring the idea of damnation or eternal felicity of a life beyond the grave."

PREDESTINATION. The Hadith calls it Qadar, the theologians Taqdir. This article of faith is added to the preceding ones and states that nothing in this world has existed or can exist without the will of Allah. This is asserted in several verses of the Koran: "And the soul will not die but with the permission of Allah."[1] ". . . the Most High . . . who makes things according to a measure, then guides them to their goal."[2] ". . . Nothing will afflict us save what Allah has ordained for us."[3] As a matter of fact, the actions of men are written on "Guarded Tablets," even before they are created. Other Koranic verses

[1] Chap. 3:144.
[2] Koran, Chap. 87:v. 3.
[3] Chap. 9:v. 51.

permit men to discuss predestination, of which the theologians have taken ample advantage.

A Muslem Persian author, Abu'l-Maali, summarises the foundations of Islamic dogma in the following passage:

"The all-powerful Divinity, with His attributes, is declared eternal; the Koran is self-existent (uncreated); Paradise and Hell are created; the existence of God and the capacity of the elect to contemplate Him with their eyes are declared real; the same is true of the punishment in the grave and the interrogation by Monkir and Nakir; the Muslems charged with capital crimes are not declared to be infidels (kafir); if they die before repenting, they submit to a punishment in hell in proportion to their sins, after which, by the intercession of the Prophet, they reach Paradise. . . . The Sunnites consider good and evil as the outcome of a preordained destiny, which, however, does not prevent the acts of men from being judged as worthy of reward or punishment; the Sunnites say that though good and evil are done with the consent of the Divine Will, nevertheless man possesses freedom of action and God has created each act in accordance with the free-will of each man; and all is provided for in the eternal science. . . . The Sunnites declare that men are helped or abandoned by God for all eternity, according to His Divine Will. Men have no other resort except to strive and to obey."

II. The Law

We have already seen that the Koran contains a series of prescriptions and interdictions, and these, developed and completed by others added at a later date, form the canonical law of Islam—that is, Shari'a, meaning "the Way to be Followed." [1] The Shari'a is concerned with the external manifestations of human action. We have also seen that Shari'a was primarily based on the Koran, added to by tradition, gradually completed through the processes of Fiqh (jurisprudence), and diversified according to different systems or rites (Madhab). Actually, it is only the works on jurisprudence (Fiqh) which are in force as law. The Koran and the collections of Hadith are only reading matter for edification. The fundamental tendency of the Shari'a was to approach the different circumstances of life from a religious point of view: the judicial implications were added later.

Attempts have been made to define the elements which constitute the Shari'a. The Orthodox distinguished three elements: obligations concerning cult (Ibadat); judicial aspects (Muamalat); and sanctions (Uqubat). The Shi'ites adopted a more detailed classification.

Human actions were divided into five categories (ahkam) and regarded from both the religious and the civil point of view.

A. From the religious point of view the distinctions were: 1—Fardh (duty), or the necessary act.[2] (Also called Wadjib.) This category comprised (1) those acts the commission of which was to be rewarded, and the omission of which was to be punished.

[1] Koran, Chap. 47:17.

[2] Fardh was in turn subdivided into two categories. One of these comprised those acts which must absolutely be done by everyone; such as prayer. The other, known as Fardh Kifaya, comprised acts which it was not necessary for everyone to perform; such as fighting in the Holy War, or praying for the dead. If some of the community carried these out, that was sufficient.

2—Mandub, recommendable acts. Their accomplishment was to be rewarded, but their omission would not be punished. 3—Mobah, permissible acts. 4—Makruh, reprehensible acts, but not punishable. 5—Haram, forbidden acts, and punishable.

This classification of human actions into five categories led to divergencies among the Orthodox rites.

B. From the civil point of view the five categories were: Sahih (right), Batil (wrong), Djaiz (permissible), Nafiz (efficacious) and Lazim (essential).

In brief, it is necessary to distinguish the two aspects of the Shari'a: that which concerns the cult; and that which comprises judicial prescriptions. We must now examine each separately.

A. Cult

The "Cult" is founded on five fundamental obligations known as Arkan-al-din, meaning the foundation stones of religion. These are the confession of faith, prayer, fasting, and the poor-rate and pilgrimage.[1]

Gaudefroy-Demombynes says: " 'The Cult,' that is the external manifestation in thought of Islam, is individual. Prayer, even when offered communally, is individual. As for pilgrimage, if one studies it closely one sees that each Muslem makes it in his own individual way."

It is important to note that any manifestation of cult must be preceded by the expression of intention (niya), without which it is not valid. This emphasis on intention is derived from Hadith which says: "Actions will be judged according to intentions, and

[1] A few authors have added the Holy War.

every man's intention will be taken into account." Another Hadith of a more recent date ascribes these words to Allah: "Show your intentions, not your works."

CONFESSION OF FAITH. Tashahhud, or bearing witness, is the confession of faith. It consists of the recitation of the formula, Shahad'a: "La ilah illa'-llah Muhammed Resul Allah," meaning: "There is no God but Allah, and Muhammed is His Prophet." This is the essential formula for conversion to Islam, plus the condition of pronouncing it integrally. The believer repeats it in solemn circumstances, especially at the approach of death. If the dying Muslem cannot pronounce it thrice, someone near him (talqin) does so for him.

The meaning of the word Shahad'a can be extended to include the fighter, who by dying in the Way of Allah, also bears witness. Those who die in the Holy War are the Shahid. The word "Shahid" also signifies witnesses who give evidence in court. The word "Shahid" is not Koranic. It was derived much later from an isolated verse. Ordinarily the Koran speaks simply of those who have died in the Way of Allah. According to Wensinck, the word Shahid used in the sense of martyr, was derived from Christian influence, and existed from very early days in the Orient. The word Shahid in the sense of martyr appears often in the Hadith (traditions). We already know that the martyr enters Heaven without being questioned by the angels of the grave, and takes his place near the throne of Allah. Later, tradition attributed to the martyr the power of intercession in favour of sinners. But, in spite of these heavenly privileges, the martyr was supposed to be longing to come back to earth and suffer martyrdom once more. According to Wensinck, this idea gave birth to a desire for self-sacrifice which Orthodox opinion tried to combat, seeing in it a tendency to suicide, which is formally forbidden by Islam. Thus the Orthodox Muslem estimated the peaceful duties, such as prayer, fasting and good acts accomplished for the love of Allah to be as meritorious as the sacrifice of one's life. This conception of the martyr was further extended, and was applied to those who died in a plague or from a similar disease, or died any kind of violent death while performing a pious duty. The woman who died in childbirth was considered a martyr. The cult of martyrs in certain Muslem countries, especially in India, was considerable.

Prayer

The Shahad'a formula was repeated several times during the ritual prayers (Salat) which has played such a great part in the early development of Islam, as well as in its later expansion. Muhammed attributed great value to it for bringing about conversions. Prayer was mentioned in the early revelation of the Koran, which is evidence of its antiquity. The Koran insists on the necessity of prayer and definitely blames those who neglect it. A restriction on the use of wine appears in one of the verses concerning prayer: "Do not engage in prayer when you are intoxicated." [1]

But it must be clearly understood that the actual form of the ritual prayer was probably fixed after the Hegira, under the influence of Hebraic ritual. Be-

[1] Chap. 4:43.

fore that, it was considered meritorious to know a great number of Koranic verses by heart, and to keep pious vigils. "Surely, your Lord knows that you pass in prayer nearly two-thirds of the night, and sometimes half of it, and sometimes a third of it, and also those who are with you." [1] Caetani says: "During the Meccan period, according to the Koran, the good Muslem needed only to believe in God and to renounce idol-worship . . . he was not at that period obliged to go through any precise form of ritual."

Eventually the Muslem had to go through five ritual prayers daily: Salat-as-Subh (the dawn prayer); Salat-as-Zuhr (the noon prayer); Salat-al-asr (the afternoon prayer); Salat al-maghrib (the evening prayer at sunset) and Salat-al-isha (the night prayer). There are many legendary explanations to account for the number of the prayers. When Muhammed ascended (isra) it is said that he received the order from Allah to prescribe fifty daily prayers. On his return he met Moses, who finding the number excessive, sent Muhammed back to Allah, who finally consented to reduce the number to five. Wensinck ingeniously finds an analogy between this scene, and the one in which Abraham intervened in favour of Sodom and Gomorrah.[2] Another traditional explanation is that the archangel Gabriel descended five times a day and performed the ritual prayers before Muhammed at their appointed times, and that Muhammed learned them from him. Hutsma supposes that there were only three prayers at first, two of which were duplicated later. Goldziher sees in this Persian influence. In short, the number was not fixed in Muhammed's

[1] Chap. 73:20.
[2] Genesis, 18:23.

time, and it is impossible to fix the exact date of its establishment.

These five daily prayers are obligatory for every healthy and able-bodied Muslem adult. The sick are exempt, but they must make up the number they have lost when they recover. Any one who neglects the prayers voluntarily is an unbeliever (kafir). But these prayers must be preceded by certain preliminaries: the faithful before approaching the presence of God must purify himself, this being probably due to Hebraic influence in Medina. Tradition ascribes these words to Muhammed: "Purity (cleanliness) is the half of faith." The Muslem Law recognizes two kinds of impurities: Hadath (minor impurity); and Djanaba (major impurity). The minor impurities are caused by contact with any unclean object, or by the natural bodily functions; the major impurities are caused by sexual relations, menstruation, nocturnal pollution and child birth.

Two kinds of purifications (Tahara) are prescribed for the two categories of impurity. Ordinary ablution (wodhou), is practised before every prayer. The water used must be legally clean. The ablution consists of washing the face, the hands, the arms up to the elbow, passing water over the head with the palm of the hand, and, finally, washing the feet.[1] In the case of lack of water the Muslem can use sand instead (Tayammum). In the case of a major impurity, the whole body must be washed with care, including the hair. Any contact with dirt while praying annuls the prayer. The body of the one who prays must be covered in accordance with the pre-

[1] Chap. 5:6.

scription of the law. Women pray with their face and hands uncovered.

Prayer is not necessarily made in a mosque. It can be made in the house or in the open air and anywhere except on a grave or in a place which is considered unclean, such as a place where animals are slaughtered. The face of the one who prays must be turned towards Mecca.[1] The space upon which a man prays must have limits set to it by something (sotra). For this purpose a prayer rug, or any piece of clean cloth, may be spread (Sadjada). The Muslem formulates, at the beginning, silently or in a loud voice, his niya (intention), declaring which particular prayer he is going to perform, i.e., morning, noon, evening, etc.

The ritual of prayer consists of the following ceremonial: (1) Standing, palms of the hands open and raised above the shoulders while "Allah Akbar" (God is Great) is pronounced. (2) Still standing, the left hand placed over the right (on the breast in the case of women, and on the middle of the body in the case of men) the first chapter of the Koran (Fatiha) is recited. (3) Leaning and touching the knees with the palms of the hand (ruku). (4) Rising (itidal) and raising the hands saying "Allah listens to the one who praises Him." (5) Putting first the knees on the ground, and the hands on the knees, and then prostration with the face touching the ground (sudjud). (6) Sitting with the knees underneath once more (djulus or qu'ud). (7) Second prostration (the second sudjud).

This series of movements, beginning with the reci-

1 Qibla: see page 158.

tation of the opening chapter of the Koran, constitute a Rak'a. The noon, afternoon, and the night prayers consist of four Rak'a;[1] the morning and sunset prayers respectively of two and three Rak'a.

After the second Rak'a, the Muslem sits with his legs under him and his hands on his knees, and formulates a special prayer in honour of Muhammed, which he finishes by turning his head to the right and to the left, saluting all believers and the guardian angels as he repeats the words: "On you rest the salutation and the mercy of Allah!"

The ritual prayer contains no particular personal demand. Its details vary according to the four Orthodox systems, with regard to whether one should pray in a loud voice or in silence, and with regard to the position of the hands. The Shi'ites differ from the Orthodox in the latter. Travellers can shorten the five prayers.

Besides this obligatory ritual of five daily prayers there are also voluntary prayers. The best known among these is the night prayer known as Salat-al-lail or Tahadjdud. This must not be confused with the last of the five daily ritual prayers. This particular night prayer resembles the night vigils of the Christians in their ancient form. It is probable that this practice was observed regularly in Islam in Muhammed's time, but it was no longer obligatory after the organisation of the five daily ritual prayers. Nevertheless it is still practised to a considerable extent, particularly in the month of Ramadan. Another voluntary prayer is the "Witr," which means

[1] In the Hanifite prayers the numbers are different: viz., 4 for the morning, 10 for the noon, 8 for the afternoon, 5 for the evening and 13 for the night.

the Odd. This consists of adding a single Rak'a to the even number of Rak'as in the night prayer. Besides this, there are some superogatory prayers called Nafl or Tatawwo, which are observed on certain occasions, such as the prayer at the time of an eclipse (kusuf khusuf), the prayer for rain (istisqa), special prayers in connection with annual religious fêtes, prayers offered for the realisation of certain events (Salai-al-Hadja), and the prayer offered before taking a grave decision (istikhara).

The prayer over the dead,[1] made before the burial, is a duty due to every dead Muslem. Whether this prayer should be made over the dead who have committed suicide has not yet been settled. The prayer over the dead is observed in the following manner: the Imam stands at the head of the coffin in the case of men, and at the foot in the case of women. After formulating the intention of the prayer he says "Allah Akbar," and recites the Fatiha; then says "Allah Akbar" again, and follows it by a prayer to the Prophet. After the third "Allah Akbar," he prays for the dead, and after the fourth for those who are assembled. He ends with the Taslima. The place where the prayer has to take place is not definitely fixed. In Java, for example, it is performed at the house of the dead; but it can take place in the mosque or at the cemetery. In North Africa the dead are carried to the cemetery, accompanied by the chanting of the borda. Doutté says: "It is no small surprise for the Orientalist to hear the first twenty verses of this Ode; it is consecrated to the Prophet, but the opening lines are addresses, as in the case of other

1 As Salat ala'l-mayyit, or Salat Al-djinaze.

Arabic Odes, to the beloved of the poet, whose death he laments." The corpse is buried in a shroud.

The ritual prayer for the dead is recited by one person only, but it is recommendable to have it recited by the assembly, preferably in the mosque. The number to recite the prayer is not fixed. The believers stand in rows, with the women behind. This common prayer, Djama'a, is presided over by an Imam, whose every attitude is ritually determined. This common prayer is a fixed duty for Fridays. It is observed at noon, and replaces the ordinary noon-prayer. According to Sahfi'ites, there must be at least forty people for it to be valid. Women do not take part in Friday prayer. It consists of a sermon (Khutba) and of two Rak'as, but usually the two Rak'as are observed before the Khutba. This sermon was formerly pronounced by the Caliph, or his representative; but with time it became the function of professional preachers (Khatib).

Friday is not necessarily a day of rest for the Muslems.

The Mosque (Masdjid, meaning the place of prostration) has been often described. It is a hall with pillars and at the back, in the centre of the wall is the "mihrab," more or less ornate. The mihrab, a niche, is in the wall, fixing the direction of Mecca (qibla), which is necessary for the validity of prayer. The Imam stands facing the mihrab. To one side of it is the mim-bar, the chair of the preacher. A raised platform is reserved for the official Koran chanters. . . . Facing the mihrab is the Sahn (the court). The four walls have ordinarily covered galleries built into them, with annexes for ritual ablutions. With regard to the form of the Mosque, according to

Marçais, its prototype is the Court of Muhammed's house. "At one extremity of the court is a shed for giving shelter to Muslems. . . . Doubtless the Christian basilicas which the Arab conquerors adapted to their cult affected the eventual position of certain parts." From one of the angles of the mosque rises the minaret, from the summit of which the Muezzin (muaddin)[1] utters the call to prayer, five times a day. Adhan (the call to prayer) is chanted in a loud voice, and the Orthodox form is composed of the following invocations: "Allah is great! I bear witness that there is no God but Allah! I bear witness that Muhammed is His Prophet! Come to prayer! Come to salvation! Allah is great! There is no God but Allah!" The number of times the invocations are repeated varies according to the system of jurisprudence to which the particular congregation may belong. The Shi'ites have inserted between the fifth and the sixth invocation the words: "Come to the best of deeds." The insertion of this invocation signifies the establishment of Shi'ism among a particular congregation.

FASTING. There is nothing to prove that in pre-Islamic days fasting (Sawm or Siyam) was not observed at Mecca. The Hanafa,[2] the ascetics preceding Islam might have very well borrowed it from the Judeo-Christians and Muhammed from them. The Meccan revelations of the Koran do not clearly speak of fasting, though there is a mention of it in the 19th chapter and the 27th verse. But after the Hegira, Muhammed instituted the Jewish fast of "Ashura"

[1] The muezzin is preferably a blind man who cannot see the inner courts and open terraces of the houses. But this applies more particularly to the Arabs.

[2] See page 26.

(meaning the tenth day).[1] This fast was observed not only during the daytimes, but from one sunset to another, just as among the Jews. But in the second year of the Hegira, owing to the tension between Muhammed and the Jews, the month of Ramadan was instituted as the period for fasting and the Ashura made an optional fast. In the eyes of the faithful, Muhammed has thus re-established the fast which had been prescribed to Christians and Jews, and which had been changed by them. But Wensinck declares that Arab paganism had already considered the month of Ramadan as sacred, and it was this which had influenced Muhammed's choice.

The fundamental regulations for a fast were formulated in the Koran, chapter 2: 183-185. Except the sick and the wayfarer who can make up for their omission by some compensation, every Muslem is obliged to fast in the Ramadan. There are other verses in the Koran which prescribe expiatory fasts.

The indispensable conditions for the validity of the fast are: the intention must be formulated each day before dawn; women in a legally impure state are exempt; it is forbidden to take anything during the fast, e.g.: aliment, water, smoke, inhalation; bleeding, the application of leeches and sexual excitation are forbidden; but if through sheer forgetfulness one puts something into one's mouth the fast is not broken.

The fast begins sometime before sunrise and ends at sunset. A meal called Fatur (break of fast) is eaten at the end of the fast. Before dawn a meal (meal of dawn) is served, after which the believer can take nothing until sunset. At the end of the fast the be-

[1] Leviticus, Chap. 16:29.

liever thanks Allah. The recitation of the Koran is recommended at the end of the day.

If a believer for no adequate reason does not fast he is liable to be imprisoned; but this remains so only in theory in the greater part of the Islamic world. The period for fasting begins as soon as the new moon is seen by two dependable witnesses, or by the proclamation of the Cadi. The manner of proclamation of the fast differs in different countries; e.g., by the firing of cannons, the hoisting of flags on minarets, etc.

Fasting is prescribed in certain other cases as well: compensation (qada), that is the making up of the omission of the fast in Ramadan; for the realisation of a wish; in relation to a ceremony prescribed by the Imam, such as for rain (istisqa); for major atonement (kafara: two months of fasting in a case when the fast is broken in Ramadan by sexual intercourse); and for minor atonement (that is, to make up for the omission of fast in Ramádan due to legal reasons). Those who are exempt are: old people, the sick, pregnant women, mothers who nurse their babies, wayfarers, and all who perform too hard labour.

Optional or supererogatory fasting is recommended for the day of Ashura, and on the Arafa for the six first days of the month of Shawwal. It is forbidden to fast during the two great annual holidays, and in time of danger. It is not recommended to fast on Fridays, Saturdays and Sundays, the Muslem, Jewish and Christian holy days.

According to current belief, fasting, especially in the month of Ramadan, is the best atonement for the sins of the year. The great theologian, Ghazali, finds in the fast a sure method of subduing the passions.

During the month of Ramadan Muslems add a prayer of twenty Rak'a to the usual nightly prayer which is made under the presidency of an Imam. At the end of Ramadan, the ending of the fast is celebrated on the first day of the month of Shawwal. This Fête of three days is called "Id-al-Fitr" or (fast-breaking holiday) or "Id-as-saghir," meaning the minor holiday. The "Id-al-Kabir" meaning the major holiday, takes place during the pilgrimage period, and lasts four days. As a matter of fact, the Minor Holiday is celebrated with more joy and enthusiasm than the Major. The Minor Holiday begins with a prayer in the open air in good weather, though it is not absolutely necessary. Special alms, Zakat-al-Fitr, meaning the alms of the break of fast, are distributed to the poor, so much for every member of the family. The exact sum per head is regulated. But this legal alms must not be confused with the poor-rate; that is, the legal tax which the believer pays according to the fourth rule of the Religious Law.

LEGAL ALMS OR THE POOR-RATE. The idea of this legal alms is derived from both the ancient Arabs and the Jews. The goods of this world are impure, but one may acquire them and enjoy them on the condition that part is restored to Allah. The word Zakat, indicating the legal alms or poor-rate, originally meant purification.

"By no means shall you attain righteousness until you spend benevolently out of what you have....[1] "Nor do they spend anything that may be spent, small or great . . . but it is written down to their

[1] Chap. 3:91.

credit. . . ."[1] But alms must not be given ostentatiously.[2]

Sadaqa, meaning spontaneous alms, is a voluntary practice, and is probably derived from the Hebrews. The distinction between the Zakat and the Sadaqa was not very precise in the Koran, nor in the collection of traditions, or even in books written by later writers on the subject. However, both Zakat and Sadaqa are to be given to the following: the poor; prisoners, both Muslem or non-Muslem; those who are in debt; those who fight in a sacred war; and wayfarers. The Sunnites do not accept Muhammed's family as having right to alms, but the Shi'ites include them.

Zakat, which is clearly prescribed in the Koran, must be paid by every Muslem who is sound in mind and body, possesses flocks, or receives a fixed annual revenue from agricultural, industrial or commercial enterprises. The Zakat to be paid is evaluated on the basis of a minimum determined revenue (nisab). This minimum is estimated for those engaged in industry and for merchants as five ounces of silver; for peasants, the minimum is five loads of dates or grain; for the stock breeder the minimum is five camels, 30 oxen, or 40 sheep.

As a matter of fact, this amounts to a tax, or rather a tithe, levied on the revenues of the rich, and divided among the needy. The rate of one-tenth can be decreased to one-twentieth, if the revenue is obtained by hard personal labour.

In principle the Zakat is paid in kind. A col-

[1] Chap. 9:121.
[2] Chap. 4:36.

lector, assisted by subordinates, collects it. For the products of the soil, he estimates directly; for other assets, the owners make declarations which are carefully examined. As Zakat was not levied on assets which had been for less than two years in the same hands, fraud must have been possible in certain cases.

Zakat lost its charitable character gradually, and became a regular tax, paid in cash. It even changed its name into Ashur in some places; in Algeria for example. As for Sadaqa, the voluntary alms, it was always very largely practised by all Muslems. The oldest and most important form of good works by Muslems is the devoting of the revenues of some particular property to pious foundations or public works. This is called Habus in Western Islam, and Waqf in Eastern Islam. These pious foundations owe their existence to legal alms. In the deed of donation it is always specified that in the case when the purpose for which the foundation has been established no longer exists, the revenue shall be given to the poor. These donations have rendered immense service to Islam by making possible the erecting of public edifices, such as universities, hospitals, soup-kitchens, etc. But with time, especially when the revenues of these foundations decreased in value, most of these pious foundations became unproductive, and the increase in their number did more harm than good. In certain countries, the principle of the inviolability of these foundations has been respected and they were then let out for an unlimited period, which, however, was in practice equivalent to selling them.

PILGRIMAGE. Though Shahada, Prayer, Fasting, and Zakat are absolute obligations, pilgrimage (Hadj) is not so absolute, since it involves so much practical difficulty in certain cases. But every adult Muslem, man or woman, must make a pilgrimage, at least once in a lifetime; that is, if he or she has the means to accomplish it.[1] It is permissible to send a representative. The following are exempt from pilgrimage: the unfit; slaves; and women who have no relative to accompany them. Other just causes for exemption are lack of means and insecurity of the route. As a matter of fact, pilgrims have always been exposed to attacks from brigands. The Meccan authorities were obliged to conclude a form of treaty with the Bedouin chiefs arranging for the security of pilgrims, in exchange of a sum called Surra. The greatest number of pilgrims to come by land are the Syrians, the Egyptians and the Iraqians. The Maghrebins and the Persians come by sea, and all manner of people belonging to every social class are found among them. Since a commission of sanitation has been established at Djidda, it has been possible to know the exact number of pilgrims who go to Mecca. It is something like 70,000 annually, which represents a very small proportion of the Islamic world. Nevertheless, its importance is still great; partly because of its political and economic consequences, and partly because of its antiquity. As a matter of fact, it represents the survival of pagan rites amalgamated with new ones. The sanctuaries visited at Mecca were considered as sacred in pre-Islamic Arabia as they are in the Muslem world today.

On page 46 we have seen Muhammed's attitude towards pilgrimage. He might have contemplated the establishment of a rival Sanctuary in Medina. Nevertheless he had greater interest in reconciling

[1] Chap. 3:96.

the Kureishite party in Medina, which was so powerful both economically and politically. Furthermore, the Meccan Sanctuary had the sanction of immemorial age. Hence sixteen or seventeen months after the Hegira, Muhammed decided in favour of Mecca as qibla—Muslems in prayer were to face Mecca instead of Jerusalem. Whereupon Hadj was established in Islam as one of the fundamental rites, analogous to the veil offered to Athena by the pilgrims of Panathenee.

A detailed description of all the rites connected with Pilgrimage is found in Gaudefroy-Demombynes's work, "Le Pèlerinage à la Mecque." These rites are divided into two categories. First, there is the Omra. That is the pilgrimage which was practised in pagan times, and has its own particular rites. It is made by the individual, and at any date he wishes, except at the time of the official pilgrimage. Second, there is the Hadj. That is the Muslem pilgrimage which must be undertaken at a given date, and in company with all other pilgrims. The Hadj takes place in the months of Dhul-Qada and Dhul-Hidjdja. The Hadj embodies the older rites, together with others more recent which are peculiar to itself.

It would be useless to describe the regional aspect of Mecca, but it would be interesting to give a short description of the principal and the most ancient sanctuary associated with it—the Kaaba. The name is derived from its shape—a thimble. But in reality it is a rectangular building with an area of 10 by 12 metres, and a height of 15 metres. It is built of grey stone found in the neighbouring mountains. The four corners are called respectively: Irakian, Syrian,

Yemenite, and the Black Stone: the first three because of their direction, and the last because of its colour. Its exterior is covered by black brocade (kiswa), a tissue woven each year in Egypt, and brought to Mecca by the Egyptian pilgrims. The sanctuary is erected on a slab of marble 25 centimetres thick. Between the 25th and 28th of Dhul-Qada the black cover is changed for white, which is the colour of the pilgrims' Ihram, their ritual dress. At the end of the Hadj, a new black cover brought from Egypt replaces the white one; and the old black one is divided into pieces and sold to pilgrims as relics. The door of the Kaaba is two metres above the ground level. A wooden ladder is in place before it, when it is open. In the interior, three columns support the roof. There is no furniture except lamps and inscriptions. The floor is of marble. A circular pavement outside (Mataf) serves for the ritual revolutions of the pilgrims around it. In front of the door is a depression in the pavement, which is regarded as the trough in which Abraham and his son Ishmael mixed the mortar when they built the Kaaba. "We made the House a resort for men and a place of security; and we appoint for you a place of prayer on the standing place of Abraham. . . ."[1] These lines are believed to allude to a stone in another small edifice in the same court where the Kaaba is built. This stone is called Maqam Ibrahim—the place where Abraham stood. Near this stone is a Mimbar (pulpit) in white marble. A small cupola shelters the well of Zemsem, probably the centre of the Sanctuary. (For the reproductions of the ensemble of other edifices see Gaudefroy-Demom-

[1] Chap. 2:125.

bynes's book and Meyerhof's "Monde Islamique.")

In the semi-circle between the wall of Kaaba and that of the outer court there is an enclosure which is considered to be the tomb of Hagar and Ishmael. Several hundred prophets are believed to have been buried there.

The Kaaba was exposed to the ravages of both time and men. It has been besieged, burnt, and the Black Stone was broken in 683. This was done during the siege conducted by the anti-Caliph Abd-Allah ben as-Zobair, who demolished and then reconstructed the Kaaba. In 929, the Karmathes [1] attacked it, and carried away the Black Stone which they restored twenty years later. In 1630, it was repaired and completely restored, as periodical inundations and climatic conditions caused considerable damage.

The Meccan territory is sacred (Al-Haram), and it is strictly forbidden to carry away any of its soil. This sacredness was recognized in the pre-Islamic period. The pilgrim before entering Mecca puts on the consecrated dress—Ihram. This consists of unsewn white cloth. One piece covers the body from the middle down to the knees; the other is wrapped round the upper part of the body, covering the back. It begins from the left shoulder and ends in a knot on the right shoulder. This costume which is pre-Islamic in design, is not different from that of ancient Hebrew women who are enveloped in a piece of cloth which covers their bodies from head to foot. The head remains bare. Sandals are permitted, though pilgrims usually go bare-footed. Before donning this sacred dress the pilgrim goes through an ablution (gosl) for major purification, and

1 See page 191.

he paints his nails with henna, perfumes his body, and shaves his hair. All this is reminiscent of the exorcizing practices of pagan days. But a man in Ihram is consecrated: he cannot hunt, pick plants, shed blood, or have sexual intercourse.

The pilgrim then recites a prayer, and formulates his intention of making the Omra and the Hadj at the same time; or only one of them, as the case may be. Then he marks the animal which he means to sacrifice (Ishar); after which he begins to say in loud voice "Laibaik!" meaning "at Thy service!" This cry is constantly repeated up to the beginning of the ceremony of the throwing of stones. Having arrived at Mecca, the pilgrim goes seven times around Kaaba (Tawaf), then enters the court of the Sanctuary and kisses or touches the Black Stone, after which other ritual circumambulations around the Kaaba take place. When the pilgrim leaves the Sanctuary, he formulates his intention of performing the ritual of Sâ'y, which consists of visiting the two hills of Mecca: Safa and Marwa. One part of the route is traversed by running, a pagan ritual which Islam explains by different legends. One of them is that Hagar, the mother of Ishmael, ran seven times between these hills in search of water for her son.

These visits to the three sanctuaries and the two hills complete the ancient rite of Omra. If the pilgrim has no further intention of making the official Hadj, he shaves his head in token of being free from further ritual interdictions. If, on the other hand, he intends to continue with the Hadj, he retains his Ihram. The Omra as we have already said, is done singly; the Hadj is performed in assembly and at a given date. The following rules are observed:

(1). In the morning of the seventh day of Dhul-Hidjdja there is a sermon for the pilgrims in the Mosque of Mecca, after which the assembly leave Mecca.

(2). On the eighth day of Dhul-Hidjdja, the procession goes to Mina and to Mozdalifa, and halts at the hill of Arafa. The plain, usually deserted, is then covered with stalls and tents, which remind one of the old pagan Arab Fairs. A great many pilgrims climb the hill, crying "Labbaik, Labbaik!" That night is spent in prayer on the hill of Arafa.

(3). The ninth day of Dhul-Hijdja is the climax of the Hadj—the day of adoration. Hutsma compares this halt at the Arafa Hill to that of the Hebrews at the Mount of Sinai.[1] After the sun crosses the meridian, an Imam ascends the Hill of Arafa on a camel, where he preaches and recites pious invocations amid general emotion. When the sun disappears behind the western hills, Iftida begins. This is a swift and somewhat confused exodus of the pilgrims towards the Moedalifa plains, to the accompaniment of rifle shots, and fireworks. The night is spent on the plains.

(4). Early in the morning of the tenth day of Dhul-Hidjdja, there is a prayer in assembly, followed by a sermon, after which the pilgrims start for Mina. The day is marked by three different rituals. Each pilgrim carries seven stones away from Moedalifa and when the assembly reaches Mina, each pilgrim throws his seven stones on one of the three stone-heaps of Mina. Each pilgrim sacrifices in person (or has someone sacrifice in his name) a sheep, a goat, or a camel, that is the animal which he has previously marked

[1] Exodus, Chap. 19:10-15.

for sacrifice. The flesh is distributed among the poor, and if anything remains from the sacrifice, it is not taken away. The sacrifice of animals, usually sheep, is carried on in all the Muslem world on the same day; for that day corresponds to the first day of the Great Holiday: Al-Id-al-Akbar. But the sacrifice is permissible during the first three days of the Great Holiday—that is from the 10th to the 13th of Dhul-Hidjdja. Finally the pilgrim shaves his hair again, and cuts his nails, both of which he carefully buries. He is then in a state of semi-consecration (Tahallul). His complete consecration is achieved after he has visited the rest of the sacred places of Mecca: Mina, Safa and Marwa.

A large number of pilgrims add to their Hadj a visit to Muhammed's tomb at Medina; and certain among them visit Jerusalem and the Mosque of Omar in that city of prophets.

The Shi'ites visit the tombs of their Imams after their Hadj.[1] The sacred cities of Shi'ism are: Kerbela, where there is the tomb of Husain; Nedjef, where Ali is buried and where every Shi'ite desires to be buried; Kazmain, near Bagdad, where the 7th and the 9th Imams are buried; Samarra, where the 10th and the 11th Imams are buried and where there is a catacomb in which the 12th Imam is supposed to have been lost.[2] These sacred cities of Shi'ism are well described by E. Aubin's "Perse d'Aujourd'hui." Besides these sacred towns of Mesopotamia, there are two other sanctuaries in Persia: Meshed, where Imam Riza is buried; Kum where there is the tomb of Fatima, the sister of Imam Riza. We will see later

1 See page 184.
2 See page 188.

how this Shi'ite cult involving the descendants of Ali led to a general cult of saints and martyrs.

To conclude, Hadj has three aspects: the religious, by which Muslems believe it to be a means of obtaining divine grace; the political, by which it brings together, at least in theory, all Muslems of the world at a given place and time; the ethnographical, by which the ancient rites of cutting the hair and nails, and burying them, and the seasonal march and processional circumambulations are all included in the Hadj.

B. Prescriptions

We have seen how the Koran contains a certain number of prescriptions, particularly in the 3rd, 4th and the 5th chapters. These principles were developed later by Fiqh (Jurisprudence), not without some influence from local customs. Since Gaudefroy-Demombynes has treated this question in his "Institutions Musulmanes," it is not necessary to go into a detailed exposition of them. Nevertheless, it would be of some interest to consider certain elements mentioned in the Koran which became the basis of the social organisation of Islam.

The Koran is, at times, not very tender to women.[1] "What! that creature who exists in ornaments, and who in contention is unable to utter plain speech."[2] Further, children and possessions are regarded as a trial to men. Nevertheless, the Koran accords per-

[1] The Koran has other passages in which kindness towards women is commanded. The best known is: ". . . And treat them kindly; for if you hate them, it may be that you dislike that in which Allah has placed abundant good" (Chap. 4:19).

[2] Chap. 43:18.

fection to two women: Asiya, the wife of Pharaoh who saved Moses; and Mary, the mother of Jesus. Muhammed himself added to this number his first wife, Khadidja, and his daughter, Fatima. The Koran reproves those who were discontented at the birth of a daughter to Muhammed.[1] It also abolished the burying alive of daughters.[2]

The Koran permits a man to take four wives. "Marry such women as seem good to you, two, three or four; but if you fear that you will act unjustly between them, then marry only one.[3] The wives to be chosen are described as "the chaste among the believers, and the chaste from among those who have been given the Book." [4] A man may also marry some from among the slaves,[5] but he must be in a position to support them. A man may not marry a daughter-in-law, except the divorced wife of an adopted son. Muhammed himself married the divorced wife of his adopted son. The wife brings no dowry. On the contrary, the husband agrees to a sum (Mihr) which he pays to his wife if he repudiates her. This money is different from that of pagan times, when the husband merely purchased his wife. In the Islamic form, it is clearly a compensation.

The Koran abolished the Levirate.[6] The widow whose husband has died may marry whoever she wishes, provided she waits for four months and ten

1 Chap. 16:58.

2 Chap. 81:9.

3 Chap. 4:3.

4 Chap. 5:5.

5 Chap. 4:24.

6 A Law of the ancient Hebrews which was practised in pagan Arabia and according to which a woman whose husband died without issue was married to the husband's brother.

days. This time is enforced to make certain whether she is pregnant or not. If a woman is merely divorced, she must wait for three menstruation periods before marrying again. But if the husband himself wants to take her back and she consents, the waiting is not necessary.

In pagan times, the right of repudiation belonged to men alone. The Koran awarded a compensation to women in the case of divorce, and she could also demand a divorce and obtain it in certain circumstances. The Koran gives definite prescriptions with regard to divorce, both with regard to the wishes of the man and the woman. A man cannot repudiate a wife more than three times. If he wishes to marry a wife whom he has repudiated three times, the marriage is permitted only if the woman has been married to another man and divorced from him.

As for the children, their state is also regulated in the case of divorce (Talaq). Pregnant women may not be divorced before their delivery. ". . . If they are pregnant, take care of them until they lay down their burden."[1] The divorced mothers "should suckle their children for two whole years for him who desires to make complete the time of suckling; and their maintenance and their clothing must be borne by the father according to usage; no soul shall have imposed upon it a duty beyond the extent of its capacity; neither shall a mother be made to suffer harm on account of her child.[2] The Koran, besides abolishing the inhuman custom of burying daughters alive, also forbids the killing of babies because of

[1] Chap. 65:6.
[2] Chap. 2:233.

poverty.[1] As for orphans, the Koran insists on careful and just dealing with regard to their property while they are minors.[2] Children themselves are also reminded of their duty to their parents in several passages, notably in the 46th chapter and the 15th verse.

Slaves are attached to a particular family. The Koran commends the kind treatment of slaves and the use of alms to buy their freedom. They must be liberated whenever they ask, provided they are worthy of it.[3]

If a man repudiates his wife by saying, "Let thy back be like the back of my mother," he cannot remarry her before freeing a slave.[4]

The principles of inheritance are too clearly treated in the 4th chapter to require any further explanation.

Every will and every promise to pay a debt must be made in the presence of two witnesses (Shahid), and the said witnesses give evidence on oath.[5] One can be released from an oath,[6] but its violation demands expiation by the feeding and clothing of ten poor people, or by freeing slaves, or by fasting.[7] Perjury is a crime and must be punished as such.[8] Evidence cannot be refused, even if it is against one's self. "O you who believe! Be maintainers of jus-

1 Chap. 17:33.
2 Chap. 4:2
3 Chap. 9:60; Chap. 24-33.
4 Chap. 58:3.
5 Chap. 5:106.
6 Chap. 66:2.
7 Chap. 5:89.
8 Chap. 24:4.

tice, bearers of witness for Allah's sake, though it may be against your own selves." [1]

An expression "Hudud Allah," meaning the limits fixed by Allah, which seems to correspond to "Sepes Legis," appears several times in the Koran, with regard to commandments as well as with regard to interdictions.[2] Penal law is fragmentary in the Koran. The four kinds of penalties which are ordained in the Koran form the basis of the penal section of the Shari'a: Kisas (Talion); Diya (ransom paid for killing); Hadd (the ne varietur penalty legally determined); Tazir, (the penalty ordained by the judge). Of these four, only the first two are defined in the Koran. In the eyes of the Shari'a, Adhab, that is to say, punishment, can be God's right or man's right. When it is man's right, it must be inflicted on the demand of the plaintiff.

But in the Koran Allah recommends that men return good for evil,[3] and promises heaven to those who forgive. Nevertheless, Diya and Kisas, which date from pagan days, have been preserved. Punishment, both under paganism and under Islam, meant purifying oneself from sin.

For the Talion, the Koran restricts vengeance to the person of the offender. ". . . Retaliation is prescribed for you in the matter of the slain: the free for the free, and the slave for the slave, and the female for the female." [4] This summary prescription leaves freedom for the interpretation of other cases. The same passage admits—entirely contrary to cus-

[1] Chap. 4:135.
[2] Chap. 2:187.
[3] Chap. 23:96.
[4] Chap. 2:178.

tom of pagan days—a reprieve of the penalty and the paying of a ransom instead; but this can only be done in the case of a first murder. The Koran, like the Pentateuch, distinguishes voluntary murder from manslaughter. In the second case, retaliation is substituted by Diya (ransom); but the wilful murderer is menaced with burning in hell.[1] The same passage of the Koran regulates the case of manslaughter. If a believer, or the member of a friendly people, is killed by accident, a slave must be freed as expiation, and a ransom paid to the family of the victim, if the family so desires. For the accidental killing of a believer, belonging to an enemy nation, only the freeing of a slave is prescribed. At a later date, Diya (ransom) was prescribed also in case of disabling any part of the body.

In brief, the Koran clearly condemns murder (Qatl), except in the case of Holy War. With regard to retaliation, the Koranic prescriptions have alleviated the harsher pagan form.

The interdiction of suicide is not clearly stated in the Koran; but it is quite precisely defined in the Hadith (tradition). Lapidation, in the case of adultery, came into practice subsequently to the Koran; the punishment prescribed in the Koran being less severe than that prescribed in Leviticus. The male adulterer must be whipped, and the adulteress shut up in a house, according to the Koran, until "death takes them away or Allah opens a way for them."[2]

On the other hand the Koran is much more severe on the thief than was paganism. The pagan considered theft as an infamy, especially when a man

[1] Chap. 4:93.
[2] Chap. 4:15.

stole from his host, or from a member of his tribe; but the thief was not punished. The Koran orders the hand of the thief to be cut off, be it a man or a woman.[1] This innovation appears to be of Persian origin. Usury is forbidden by several verses in the Koran.[2]

Alimentary interdictions appear in a series of passages in the Koran, but Khamr (wine) was not immediately forbidden. Lammens says that with very little exception the soil of Arabia is not favourable to wine-culture, and wine was probably imported from Syria and Iraq, and sold to the tribes by the Christians and Jews. In the time of Muhammed, even the people of Mecca and Medina drank wine and practised gambling, which were hindrances to religious observances. Hence, the Koran which speaks of wine as a divine gift in Chapter 16:69, warns the believers against both wine and gambling in chapter 2:219. Both were definitely prohibited in chapter 5:90. Nevertheless, the Bacchanalian scenes described by Muslem poets show that the prohibition of wine was not strictly observed.

Other prohibitions with regard to alimentation are grouped in the Koran in Chapter 5:3, and consist of; dead animals (Maita); blood; Swine; strangulated animals; animals killed by accident or felled; and animals partly eaten by beasts. It appears that even in pagan times Arabs avoided eating the blood of animals because of ritualistic prohibition. It is not necessary to invoke Jewish influences here.

The same verse ends by the interdiction of dividing up sacrificed animals by "The Consultation of

[1] Chap. 5:38.
[2] Chap. 2:275.

Arrows," by Maisir, or by "raised stones." According to commentators, Maisir signifies all kinds of gambling. The Consultation of Arrows (Azlam), was a particular form of gambling belonging to pagan days. In those days the meat of a camel was divided into a certain number of parts, and distributed to the gamblers who drew arrows from a bag. This form of gambling with arrows was a favourite with the pagan Arabs, who at times lost all their possessions, even betting the members of their families. The "raised stones" (Ansab) represented the idols of the pagans, around which the pagan Arabs circumambulated ritually, after offering a libation. The circumambulations around the Kaaba and the Black Stone are mere survivals from those days.

These idols, the adoration of which the Koran forbids to Muslems, bring us to a much discussed question in Islam: the prohibition of the Sura on images. And this prohibition is not peculiar to Islam. The Eastern Church, under Leo III, passed through that phase with the Paulicians. Contrary to current belief, this particular interdiction is not formally defined in the Koran; but its origins are there in passages where it is said that Allah is the Modeler of all things.[1] The same idea occurs in the old Hebraic literature, where Jehovah is called the Potter. From this conception tradition drew the following conclusion: the makers of images are imitators of Allah, and therefore they must be punished. As a matter of fact, the law, elaborated from Sunna and Hadith, prohibited the production of images of living creatures, though it did not object to those of trees and inanimate objects; for example,

[1] Chap. 3:5.

such as one sees in the mosaics of the Mosque at Damascus. Certain jurists drew a distinction between the effigies of animals made on such articles as rugs and cushions, articles which one treads upon, and the effigies of animals made on walls or on dresses. They permitted the former and prohibited the latter. Puppets were also forbidden; but this prohibition was even less observed than the prohibition of wine. In spite of these laws, however, Muslem art multiplied the figures of men and animals; for instance, such as are found in the baths of Amra in Transjordania; among the wooden carvings of Maristan of Kalaoun in Cairo; and, of course, the lions of the fountain of the Alhambra in Granada. Besides, illuminators of manuscripts produced popular images of the Prophet and the members of his family. Painting is a recognised art among Muslems in certain countries, and photography is in use everywhere.

The origin of another Muslem practice is attributed to the Koran, which does not, however, contain a single word which refers to it: that is, Khitan, meaning circumcision. Snouck Hurgronje remarks judiciously, "For a large number of non-Muslems and the uneducated masses of Islam, abstention from eating pork and circumcision have become the criteria of Islam." Circumcision, which at the moment is a custom which is passing away in certain Muslem countries, was practised in pagan Arabia, as we know from its ancient poetry, rites and traditions. Madhabs (rites) do not agree exactly about the way it must be performed. In Java and Sumatra, it implies only excision. Circumcision takes place generally between the ages of 7 and 15. To this small operation, however, other rites have at times been added; such as, the first cutting of the hair (aqiqa), the filing of the teeth, and the ceremony which includes the study of the Koran—rites which were practised long before Islam.

CHAPTER V

Religious and Philosophical Evolution

ISLAM changed and evolved like any other religion. We have already noted how in Muhammed's lifetime Orthodoxy had resisted every germ of dissent and how immediately after his death dissent had arisen. There were three principal causes for this.

(1). The prophetic tendencies characteristic of the Semitic races, of which the Hebrew Prophets of the old days were a sign, and which tendencies among the Arabs were evident in the Hanifs, the predecessors of Muhammed, and in the number of false prophets who sprang up after his death.

(2). The controversies centring around the Caliphate, which gave rise to Shi'ism and Kharidjism.

(3). Controversies with regard to the nature of the Divinity, which gave rise to mystical and rational schools of thought.

The sects in Islam were the result. It is necessary to remind the reader that Rites and Sects should not be confused. We know that the orthodox Muslems are attached to four different rites, or judicial systems, known as Madhab, these being the Malekites, Shafi'ites, Hanbalites and Sunnites (page 121). For example, a sect is a different conception, is known as Firqa, and means a party, the members of the Firqa are opposed to consensus (Idjma) on fundamental questions, and are therefore separated from

Orthodox Islam, and belong to a dissentient church.

Goldziher has tried to prove that "The multiplicity and diversity of sects attributed to Islam is much greater than a sane appreciation of reality would permit." According to Hadith (tradition), Judaism has 71 virtues, Christianity 72, and Islam 73. Muslem theology has transformed these 73 virtues of Islam into 73 branches. Through some misunderstanding, the virtues were interpreted as sects, and it was believed that of the 73 only one, that of the Sunnites, would escape everlasting fire. But this Draconian interpretation was opposed by a more tolerant one later: only one sect, that of Zindiqs, would be cast into hell.

On the other hand, the number of 70, that is the multiple of 7, and the number 73 has a sacred significance in Asia. This seems to have had an astronomical origin. 70 is one-fifth of the Lunar year, and 73 one-fifth of the Solar year. This conception, probably coming from ancient Persia, passed to the Jews; for instance, the seventy weeks mentioned in the Book of Daniel. And from the Jews it passed to the Christians and the Muslems. Applied comparatively to the different religions, it gave birth to a tradition in Islam that the religion which had the greatest number of sects would be final.

PROPHETIC TENDENCIES. False prophets had already appeared in Arabia in the days of the first Caliph, Abu-Bekr. It may be useful to summarise their teachings so far as we know them from the records left by historians. Among the first, was Tulaiha. There remain fragments of his writings, from which it is evident that they were imitations of the Koran, more like a parody of it. Abandoned by his partisans, he was castigated by the Muslems, after which he took refuge in Syria.

Also there was the prophetess, Sadja, who led her tribe in rebellion by her preaching to them in a rhythmic prose after the manner of the Kahins, that is the soothsayers of the pagan days. Her followers were dispersed, but she fled to Yamama, where she joined a much more formidable personality: the false prophet, Mosailama.

Mosailama belonged to the tribe of Banu-Hanifa, which was partly Christian and principally occupied with agriculture. It seems that he proposed to base his religion on Christian ideas, calling his God "Rahman," which means the Merciful. This may have been derived from a Christian source, but the word also appears in the Koran.[1] The desperate resistance of his followers continued even after his fall on the battlefield.

Another false prophet called Al-Aswad, meaning "The Black" arose in Yemen and captured Sanaa, the capital, where the half-castes, the children of Persian conquerors by native wives, were in a majority. Al-Aswad was betrayed by his wife, formerly the widow of the Persian governor. He was assassinated. He seems less like a false prophet than an agent of Arab penetration in a country where Persian influence was dominant. Henceforward, politics and religion were to be closely interrelated.

Political influence on religious movements manifested itself much more openly in the question of the succession of the Caliphate. Immediately after Muhammed's death, difficulties and disorder with regard to the succession had become apparent in the

[1] Page 105.

Muslem community. Omar's energetic attitude, which imposed Abu-Bekr as the first Caliph, had restored order; and in Omar's time Orthodoxy had remained secure. But in Othman's time conflicts between the two branches of the Kureishite family became acute, and it reached its apogee during Ali's reign. With Ali dissent, with clear political aims, manifested itself in Islam.

KHARIDJISM. The oldest of these movements is Kharidjism. It was the outcome of the arbitration between Ali and Moawiya which suspended the Battle of Siffin.[1] A group of fighters on Ali's side challenged the right of man to judge, and declared that "Judgment belongs to God alone." They retired to the village of Hazura in the environs of Kufa, and took the name of Harurites. When the result of the arbitration was made public, a large number of Ali's partisans left Kufa and joined the dissentients. Their name, Kharidjite, is derived from the word Kharadja, which means to come out. Non-Arabs who wished to claim lost territory joined them and increased their numbers. We know already with what difficulty Ali managed to suppress them before his assassination. Under the Omayyads, in spite of the vigorous and methodical administration of Moawiya, the Kharidjites stirred up revolts, notably in Kufa and in Basra, which were only suppressed after much bloodshed. The Kharidjite martyrs became, like those of the Shi'ites objects of a cult. But the Kharidjites added to this cult the pagan obligation of vengeance. Years of guerilla warfare followed; the Kharidjites being as excellent riders as the Parthian cavalry, they infested lower Mesopotamia and took

[1] Page 57.

refuge, when defeated, in the Persian mountains. They fought against Ibn-az-Zobair as well as against the Omayyad governors.[1] After the death of the Caliph Yazid, the Kharidjites split into several secondary sects, the best known among them being the Azraqites, the Sufrites, and the Ibadites, which are also known as Abadhiya, or Ibadhiya.

The Azraqites were a fanatical sect which believed in the massacre of all non-Muslems who refused to be converted. Further they threatened the unity of the Caliphate by establishing a state of their own in Southern Persia. After a series of campaigns, they were exterminated towards the end of the seventh century. About the same time the Kharidjites invaded Southern Arabia.

Among the Kharidjite sects, the Sufrites were the first to make a systematic exposition of their religious principles. They took up a position mid-way between the Azraqites and the Ibadites, advocating a temporary abstention from religious war against other Muslems, permitting dissimulating of their faith as a measure of prudence (Taqiya); and forbidding the murder of the children of the infidels. Their moral code was also less brutal than that of the Azraqites. During the reign of the last Omayyads, the Sufrites were dispersed over the Islamic world as far as Maghreb, where, together with the Ibadites, they prepared a general rising of the Berbers. Maswueray says: "The Kharidjite revolt against Damascus was a repetition of the old struggle of Africa against Rome and Byzantium. . . . Two thirds of Africa were Islamised through the Kharidjites, but ironically enough, were also,

[1] Page 61.

through them, encouraged to rise against Orthodox Islam."

The Ibadites, representing the more moderate and tardy elements of Kharidjism, eventually absorbed the Sufrites. Their revolt in Arabia, under the last Omayyad Caliph, unwittingly contributed to the Abassid success. Expelled from the sacred cities, they maintained themselves in Oman, and spread on one side into Zanzibar, and on the other into North Africa, where, together with the Sufrites, they encouraged the Berbers to abandon Orthodoxy. It is well known how the Berbers, tired of the superior attitude of the Caliph's governor, were ready to take up any doctrine which advocated absolute equality among Muslems. With this, Dynastic ambition began to show itself. The Ibadites and the Sufrites disputed Kairuan, where finally an Ibadite of Persian origin called Abu Rustem became governor. Before long, Kharidjites held the whole of North Africa, and threatened to separate it from the Empire. The Abassid governors established order in 772 only after a series of difficult campaigns. Nevertheless, the Ibadite sect of Kharidjism did not disappear from Maghreb. The Rustamid Dynasty maintained itself in Tahert for more than 130 years; that is, until the Fatimid triumph. From 909 onwards, the Fatimids obliged the Ibadites to take refuge in the Sahara. Further division into political and religious sects took place among the Ibadites, but their communities are still flourishing at Djerba in Djebel-Nefusa, at Ouargla, and more particularly at Mzab, where they have founded several towns and irrigated the desert. The Maghrebian communities maintain communications with the Ibadite communities of

Oman and Zanzibar. The Imam of Maskat is an Ibadite.

Ibadism to-day represents the last vestige of Kharidjism. Its offensive power was first broken by Haddjadj and his lieutenants, and the uncompromising nature of its doctrine brought its political effectiveness to an end towards the middle of the 8th century. After that, its energy was concentrated on commercial activities, and on the study as well as the composition of theological, judicial and historical works. As a matter of fact, Kharidjism was not hostile to intellectualism; for quite a number of scholars, poets and orators under the Abassids were from among the Kharidjites.

The Kharidjite doctrine was never codified, a fact which led to many variations among its numerous sects. Nevertheless, the Kharidjites played a part in the development of Muslem theology, especially with regard to Mutazelism, with which we will deal later. Generally speaking, the Kharidjites may be called the Puritans of Islam. From the earliest days they rejected the 12th chapter of the Koran because of the love story of Joseph with the Egyptian, a theme which other Muslem poets of Persia and Turkey had used a great deal. Kharidjism upheld the infallibility of the Koran, the uncreated word of Allah which contained all science, and which must be literally interpreted. Although less rigorous in regard to adultery than the Orthodox who had demanded the lapidation of adulterers, they were severer on questions of cult and faith. While the Orthodox purified themselves only externally by ablutions before the ritual prayer, the Kharidjites demanded an absolute purity of conscience. For them faith was non-existent if it did not express itself in acts, and they did not admit any degrees in faith. Whoever committed a cardinal sin lost his standing as a Muslem, and must, according to their extremists, be exterminated with all his family. In practice, they condemned all kinds of luxury, and forbade music, gambling, smoking and alcoholic drinks.

But it was the political theory of Kharidjism which had a strong influence over the destinies of Islam. All Kharidjites were unanimous on the subject of the Caliphate, a question which divided Islam more than any other into religious sects. Kharidjism believed that every Muslem, even a slave was eligible for the Caliphate or the Imamate, regardless of his colour or social position, provided he was capable of carrying out justice, and was a man of pure morals and sincere faith. Further, the Muslem community had the right to depose him if he proved himself incapable, just as was done to Ali after the Battle of Siffin. The Kharidjites recognised only the first two Caliphs —Abu-Bekr and Omar. They upheld the elective system of the Caliphate, and rejected the Hereditary system. On this point they were in complete contradiction to the Shi'ites, the partisans of Ali, who believed in a theoretical state founded on divine rights. Hence, while Shi'ism, in its evolution, enriched the adventitious elements in the Islamic doctrines, the Kharidjites stood for the restoration of an ideal state where justice would reign, a state which had become impossible because of the vastness of the Muslem Empire. Kharidjism also added the idea of Mahdi.

MORDJISM. The Mordjists, a moderate sect, took up a position between the Kharidjites and the

Shi'ites. Their name, derived from the Arabic word Mordjiya, means "those who adjourn." Contrary to Kharidjism, which had declared faith non-existent if not expressed in action, an attitude which contained a criticism of the Omayyads, the Mordjists declared conduct and practice as secondary: to them, a believer with bad conduct was better than an unbeliever with a virtuous character. In brief, the Mordjists refused to judge a man by his actions, leaving that to Allah. This part of their doctrine was naturally meant to legitimize the Omayyads. But their opportunism found favour neither with the Kharidjites nor with the Shi'ites.

SHI'ISM. It is necessary to correct a popular error with regard to Shi'ism before proceeding to a study of it. It is generally supposed in speaking of Sunnism and Shi'ism, that the latter does not admit the Sunna of the Prophet. On the contrary, the Shi'ites base their doctrine exclusively on the Sunna as recorded by the members of the Prophet's family. The difference between the Shi'ite and the Sunnite Orthodoxy on this question is that the latter also admits the authority of the companions of the Prophet. The Shi'ites are the partisans of the family of the Prophet, and exclude all other authority. Their very name is taken from a root which means "partisan." Hence the collection of Hadith (tradition) of the Shi'ites, which is called Akhbar, contains the majority of the Hadith found in the collection of the Sunnites, known merely under the name of Hadith. The main difference between the two collections lies in the personnel of the agents who have transmitted the Hadith.

If we put aside the authority of the doctrines of

the Shi'ites and the Sunnites, the divergencies between their liturgy are only secondary. Nevertheless, there is an important difference between them with regard to the matrimonial law. Shi'ism admits temporary marriage, which is now gradually becoming obsolete. This marriage, which was practised among the pagan Arabs, was tolerated by Muhammed in the early days of his mission. The temporary marriage was a contract between a man and woman for a definite period, at the expiration of which it became automatically void. It was finally abolished by Omar whose authority the Shi'ites did not accept; hence, they continued to tolerate the practice.

However, one must not deduce from this that the Shi'ites are less rigorous than the Sunnites in other respects. On the contrary, they interpret, for example, the Koranic verse "the Polytheists are impure" in its literal sense, and avoid all contact with non-Muslems. In fact, they carry this to an extreme by considering every receptacle used by a non-Muslem as polluted, and by breaking it. This rigorism is particularly the case with the Mutawali sect, the Shi'ites of Syria, who call themselves Djafarites. The word is derived from the name of the sixth Imam, Djafar, who codified the Fiqh according to the Imamite Rite.

Another common error in regarding Shi'ism is that it is believed to be of Iranian origin. This is not the case. Their very name has an Arabic origin, and as for their doctrine, certain elements of it, especially its theocratic basis and the belief in the hidden Imam, seem to have been influenced by the Judeo-Christians. In the details of the doctrine, Zoroastrianism, Neo-Platonism and Manicheism have had a formative part. The principal cause of the error which attributes an Iranian origin to Shi'ism arises from the fact that Shi'ism was adopted as the state religion in Persia in the 16th century.[1] Among the causes which led to the spread of Shi'ism in Persia a certain tradition must be mentioned: Husain, the son of Ali and the martyr of Kerbela, married the daughter of the last Sasanid king of Persia, who had been taken a prisoner during the conquest. This tradition conferred a double legitimacy in Persia on the descendants of Ali and as legitimacy is a basic doctrine with the Shi'ites, they consider Ali and his family unjustly deprived of their rights. In fact, they go as far as to accuse the Sunnites of having suppressed those Koranic verses and traditions which establish Ali's rights to the Caliphate. According to a well known Shi'ite tradition, the Prophet, in the presence of his several companions, recognised Ali as his successor. The anniversary of this investiture is kept as a holiday under the name of Id-al-Ghadir, and recorded as such in the Shi'ite calendar. To this they add the holiday of Ashura, the anniversary of the martyrdom of Husain and his family at Kerbela.[2] For Shi'ism, Ali and his twelve descendants are the true Caliphs, though they are called Imams. This use of the word Imam has a different significance from when it is used by the Sunnites. The Orthodox Sunnite considers the Imam to be a temporal and the spiritual chief, elected or nominated by the Muslem community; that is, by human beings. For the Shi'ite, the

[1] Page 245.

[2] The word Imam, in ordinary usage designates the person who presides over prayers and the other rituals in the Muslem community.

Imam is heir to the Prophet and to his mission; therefore he is appointed by divine will, and according to one Shi'ite tradition, this appointment was brought about by Muhammed's intervention. The Imam is an Imam because of a mysterious emanation peculiar to him from the time of Adam, and which he passes on to his successor. In brief, the Sunnite means a chief, when he says Imam; while the Shi'ite means a pontiff. The extremist Shi'ites evolved a notion of the Imam in direct opposition to that of Kharidjite theory. Abu'l-Maali says:

"The Shi'ite doctrine can be summed up as follows: The twelve Imams were infallible. Each one of them could work miracles; each one of them before dying nominated his successor; and this continued until the advent of Imam Hasan-Ibn-Ali-Askari. This last Imam will in turn transmit the Imamate to his son, by saying: 'Here is the Mahdi, the Master of Time!' Actually Imam Hasan was born in 869 in Samarra, and there is a cave where he is supposed to have disappeared underground. Pilgrims still go there on pilgrimages."

Hence, Shi'ism unites in Ali and his descendants the principles of hereditary royalty, as well as the principle of prophecy; therefore the existence of the Imam for all time is a necessity for them. Ali's direct descent stopped at the twelfth Imam; but according to Shi'ism this last Imam has not died. He has only retired to a secret place, where he is biding his time.

Further, because of their divine emanation, the Imams are sinless and infallible, attributes which are reserved exclusively to Prophets by the Sunnites. From this idea of the infallibility of the Imam Goldziher draws the following conclusion: Sunnism is a church based on consensus (Idjma), while Shi'ism is a church based on authority. This is probably the vital difference between the two doctrines. But, Sunnism believes that since the organisation and the establishment of the Orthodox Schools, Idjtihad—that is, personal opinion based on a free discussion of the principles of the Law—has been replaced by a docile acceptance of authority (Taqlid); while, though Shi'ism does not accept consensus in matters of dogma because of its inherent belief in the weakness of human reason, it admits Idjtihad as practised by the Shi'ite doctors of Law. The Shi'ite doctor of law is an organ of the hidden Imam; therefore, whatever he says is inspired by the Imam. This has invested the Shi'ite doctors of law with greater freedom of thought and a superior authority than those of the Sunnites, who are known as Ulema. The Shi'ite doctor of law is called Mudjtehid; and in the old days he had even the right to censure the Shah. The great Mudjtehids live in the sacred cities of Shi'ism.[1]

It is, after all, only natural that the Caliphs could not favour the spread of such a doctrine. Its partisans were therefore suppressed, and the Shi'ite Church became a persecuted Church. The Omayyads, concerned with their temporal power, saw in Ali's partisans an opposition which stood for the spiritual power of Islam. As for the Abassid Caliphs, the Shi'ites never forgave them for having used Shi'ism so craftily to overthrow the Omayyads.[2] In spite of the honours heaped on certain of the Imams, the Abassids were suspicious of Shi'ism itself, seeing an element of opposition in its perpetual protest

[1] Page 163.
[2] Page 66.

against the legitimacy of the Abassid Caliphs. This atmosphere of suspicion, threatening persecution made the Shi'ites lead a hidden life; they concealed their beliefs and would often forego the prescriptions of their cult. This tendency, which was a mental restriction known as Taqiya or Kitman, was not peculiar only to Shi'ism and there are allusions to it in the Koran.[1] There were times when even the Hanifite, the Sunnite and the Kharidjite found the practice of Taqiya permissible. But it was practised by the Shi'ites to such a degree that in spite of the reservations made by theoreticians, the hidden life became a distinctive characteristic of the extremist Shi'ite. It is only fair to add that this mental restriction was created by circumstances, and not as the result of a free choice on the part of the Shi'ites. It was often a question of avoiding bloodthirsty reprisals.

Reduced to renouncing their political activities, the Shi'ites, like the Kharidjites, gave themselves up to elaborating their doctrine in secret, and multiplying into numerous sects. Some of these sub-sects afforded them the opportunity of political influence, which they had hitherto sought in vain.

But Shi'ism, before the days of its temporal success, had already created its outlook through suffering, giving rise to the idea of Passion and Redemption.[2] The Imam must necessarily die in martyrdom, and historians tell us that in actual fact all the Shi'ite Imams met a violent death. The Shi'ite be-

[1] Chap. 3:27; Chap. 16:110.

[2] It was this idea which gave birth to dramatic works in Persian which are reminiscent of the Christian Mystery plays of Mediaeval days. They contain the usual popular religious characters and sublime beings who appear from time to time.

lieves that the presence on earth of an Imam is necessary to the world, and that therefore the last Imam is alive and is hiding somewhere, and that some day he will re-appear. Meanwhile, during this absence, which is called Ghaiba, the Shi'ite community considers itself governed by the invisible Imam, and every Shi'ite gives his oath of allegiance to him. In 1910, the Persian Parliament opened with an oath of allegiance to this invisible Imam. Though the great majority of the Shi'ites believe in the return (Radja) of the invisible Imam at some future time, their sects differ among themselves as to the number of the Imams that lived and the person of the last one. While the Duodecimian Imamites believe in twelve Imams, the Zaidites believe only in five, and the Ismaelians, or septimians, only in seven.

The Zaidite Shi'ites are nearest to Orthodoxy. This sect founded an independent and elective Imamate in Yemen, which has held its own since 860; and that in spite of the Ottoman invasion. Zaid, from whom the sect derives its name, was that grandson of Husain who revindicated the rights of the Alids and was consequently killed by Omayyad soldiers in 740. Zaidites reject temporary marriage, and do not believe in the divine emanation of the Imam; further, they do not believe in the return of the invisible Imam. For the Zaidites, since the death of Zaid, the Imamate has been either elective or hereditary.

On the other hand, for the majority of Shi'ite sects, a belief in the return of the invisible Imam is a dogma. The twelfth Imam, Muhammed, born in 837, disappeared mysteriously, and it is believed that it is he who will come back at the right moment to play his part as the Mahdi. Imamism became the official religion of Persia.[1] Shi'ism owes this triumph to the Samanian tolerance which made it possible for Shi'ism to come into the light in the early part of the 10th century. With the entry of the Buids into Bagdad half a century later, Shi'ism won the day. It was then that the four books of Shi'ite traditions were collected as counterpart to the six books of Sunnite traditions. Those Imamites who believe their four books, together with the Koran, to be the basis of their law without the Idjtihad, are called Akhbari (Traditionalists); but the majority of the Shi'ites are Usuli, that is, partisans of speculative methods. We have already mentioned the independence of mind of the Persian Mudjtehids.

Hence, while the Zaidites believe the Imam to benefit from divine guidance without being necessarily infused by some divine emanation, the Imamites believe him to be literally created of a luminous substance. To the extremist sects, this immanence (hulu) is complete and absolute: the Imam is created of the divine, and is divine.

Before examining the doctrinal activities of the extremist sects, it would be well to consider a little further this idea of the return of the invisible Imam; for it was the origin of certain of the Mahdist movements.

MAHDISM. The conception of the Mahdi so tardily taken up by the Sunnites lacked precision.[2] The Mahdi was at first supposed to be Jesus, and then Muhammed himself, to whom is ascribed the following words: "No other Prophet after me." Casanova took up the latter conception. The Mahdi

[1] Page 245.
[2] Page 135.

must bear the name of Muhammed, and be his re-incarnation. This notion of re-incarnation became very dear to Shi'ism.

The Koran contains a series of verses [1] referring to the Day of Judgment, which, if they are not indirectly derived from, are at least reminiscent of the Apocalypse.

These verses gave rise to numerous Hadith, one of which ascribes to Muhammed the following prophecy: "The world will not come to an end before a man of my family, bearing my name, rises and leads my people." These words naturally opened a way for all manner of impostors.

Extreme Shi'ism adopted the Mahdist idea, and used it in favour of Ali, who, as a member of the Prophet's family was to become the Mahdi; or, failing him, some member of his family. Extremists even transformed Ali into a divinity who commanded the thunder, a divinity reminiscent of the Hindu god, Indra.[2] Gradually it came to be believed that the Mahdi was not to be a member of Muhammed's family.

Obaid-Allah took advantage of these traditions to establish the Fatimid Dynasty in the early part of the 10th century.[3] Two centuries later a new Mahdi appeared in the person of Ibn Tumart, the founder of the Almohad Dynasty.[4] Other attempts of the kind failed in Maghreb; as they did in Egypt, where two Mahdis arose, one against Napoleon in 1799, and the other against the English in 1883.

1 Chap. 77:7; Chap. 54:1.

2 See Ibn Khaldun, Vol. 1, page 404.

3 Page 73.

4 See page 221.

Further, the Messianic idea appears in every epoch of Islamic history. An example of it is recorded by Ibn Khaldun among the people of Hilleh in Mesopotamia, who believed implicitly in the return of a member of Ali's family who had long ago died. Every evening they would lead a harnessed horse to the house where he had died, and call upon his name. Later, under the reign of the Safevids of Persia, two harnessed horses were kept ready, one for the Master of Time, and the other for His Vicar, who was to be Jesus. There are many more such examples around the belief in the coming of the Mahdi. The important point to remember is that the belief was made sometimes to serve socialistic and sometimes theocratic ideals; these two trends of thought belonging respectively to the two extreme groups of Shi'ism, namely, the Karmaths and the Ismailians.

KARMATHS AND ISMAILIANS. These two extreme sects (Gholat) recognise only the first seven Imams. That is their essential belief, and they are sometimes called Septimians. Their rejection of the last five Imams is for the following reason. The sixth Imam, Djagfar Sadiq, deeming his eldest son unworthy of the Imamat, dispossessed him in favour of his second son. Unlike the Imamites in general, the Ismailian sect did not accept the deposition of the eldest son Ismail, and refused to believe in the rumours of his death. The descendants of the sect remained faithful to Ismail, and spread their doctrine throughout Persia and Syria by their missionaries called the Da'i, who preached an allegorical interpretation of the Koran.

For a century the activity of the sect remained mainly religious. But one of their missionaries, Abd-

Allah, deviated towards a political aim. Helped by other Da'i, he was able to give an extraordinary impetus to Ismailian propaganda. As a matter of fact the Da'i, Hamdaan Qarmath won over the peasants and the workers of Mesopotamia to the belief in the invisible Imam, a belief which satisfied their egalitarian tendencies, and gave life to the organisation, the members of which were admitted by a graded initiation. The same principle is found in the Western organisation of Free-Masons. An exposition of the Karmath doctrines is found in Massignon's article, entitled "E. I. Karmates." The movement spread from Mesopotamia into Arabia, and culminated in a vulgar form of communism, accompanied with excesses which compelled the intervention of other Ismailian sects, notably the Fatimids.

For their part, the rise of the Fatimids was briefly as follows: While Hamdaan Qarmath was preaching in Mesopotamia, another Da'i, Abu Abd-Allah was rousing great enthusiasm among the Berbers of Ifrikiya by announcing the approaching advent of the Invisible Imam. It is impossible to give here a detailed account of how Obaid-Allah, the supposed Mahdi, arrived in Africa and was thrown into prison in Sidjilmassa. Da'i Abd-Allah then saved the Mahdi, together with the Berbers of Ketama who had risen against the Aghlabids, placing Obaid-Allah on the throne as the Amir of the Believers, the descendant of Ali and Fatima. Once masters in Ifrikiya, the Fatimids had directed their ambitions towards the East, from where they had originally come. Seventy years later they implanted Ismailism, at least officially, in Egypt, where it lasted for two centuries.

To conclude, it seems that the Karmathian sect

of Ismailians made use of their doctrine of the invisible Imam for the promotion of a social revolution; while the Fatimids, on the other hand, rejected this socialistic tendency and utilised both the Karmathian propaganda and the doctrine of the invisible Imam for purposes of political domination.

The legitimacy of the Fatimid Caliphs has been often contested by Muslem historians. Did they really descend from Ali and Fatima? But when one examines with care the basis of the Ismailian doctrine, one comes to the conclusion that the hereditary transmission of the Imamate from one to the other, which is essential to other Imamites, has no importance in the eyes of the Ismailians. The Imamites insist on the direct line from Ali, and on the designation of each Imam as such by his predecessor; but the Zaidites had already come to believe that every partisan of Ali had a right to the Imamate for the purpose of defending Shi'ism. Both the Karmathian and the Fatimid sects reduced the Imamate to what Massignon describes as: "an imperative mandate conferred on a new titulary among the initiated, by a sudden illumination of his intellect." From this point of view the legitimacy of the Fatimids becomes a secondary matter. They could make use of this idea, and proclaim themselves Imams as the beneficiaries of a divine emanation, then wait for the day when one among them, namely, Hakem, would be accepted as God.

Another point of interest in the evolution of Ismailian doctrine is the continual intervention of the number seven which had a sacred significance in their eyes. This might have been due to Gnostic influence. However, Ismailism established five degrees as existing between man and God. With the inclusion of man and God, the number of degrees became seven. The five intermediary degrees were: Universal Reason; Primal Matter; Universal Soul; Space, and Time. Universal Reason was incarnated successively in seven Prophets, namely, Adam, Noah, Abraham, Moses, Jesus, and Muhammed the Prophet, and, the seventh, Muhammed the son of the seventh Imam, Ismail. This marks very clearly the abysmal difference between Orthodox Islam and Ismailism, though the allegorical interpretation of the Koran and the belief in metempsychosis already constituted essential divergences between the two. While Orthodoxy considered the Prophet Muhammed as the last, and believed that the Mahdi could only consummate his mission upon earth at the end of the world, Ismailism superseded the mission of Muhammed in favour of that of a new prophet. Further, each of these seven prophets was followed by seven Imams, the first of which was always contemporary with the prophet himself. To the first five prophets the following contemporary Imams were attached: Seth, Sem, Ishmael, Aaron, Simon Peter; and, in the case of Jesus, the last being John the Baptist. To Muhammed, Ali was attached; followed by his first six successors, down to the seventh prophet, Imam Ismail. But Imam Ismail's son, Muhammed, opens the seventh prophetic cycle. His Imams are his missionaries, the Da'i, beginning with the first Ismailian missionary, and Abd-Allah, then followed by his two sons, and the first Fatimid Caliph, Obaid-Allah, who was the fourth Imam.

One can easily imagine the consequence of this arithmetical symbolism, where one may see traces of the neo-Platonian doctrine of Emanation. The Fatimid Caliphs end the seventh cycle of the Imams, the first of which is the last Prophet. Goldziher says: "The logical Ismailians could not be satisfied merely with the supreme temporal manifestation of the Universal Reason in the person of the Fatimid Imam. The prophetic cycle had to be closed. And in 1017 they believed the time had come for the Fatimid Caliph, Hakem, to declare himself as the incarnation of God." With this, Ismailism gave birth to the Druze sect. The name is derived from Darazi, one of the familiars and propagandists of Caliph Hakem.

The Druzes lived in Hauran, the mountainous region of Syria, which had been the scene of Darazi's preaching. They waited for and believed in, the return of Hakem, just as the Imamites waited for the return of the invisible Imam. Hakem, their divinity, they considered unique, and without attributes. The number seven intervenes in the form of seven principles or precepts. They admitted Taqiya (mental restriction) much more than did the Shi'ites, and believed in metempsychosis. They did not preach their doctrine; its rituals were known only to the initiated.

The deification of Hakem by the Druzes was opposed by another secret doctrine which had established itself a little time before, the doctrine of the Nosairis, who are more often known as the Ansaryes or Alauites. The hostility between these two sects lasted for centuries. While the Druzes deified Hakem, the Nosairis (as also a more recent sect called the Ali-Ilahi) deified Ali. They said: "The divine nature of Ali is eternal: though in appearance he is our Imam, in reality he is our god." They believed in a Trinity comprising Ali, Muhammed and Salman. To them, Muhammed was only an emanation of Ali, and Salman his harbinger. Without going into a detailed description of their doctrine one may note the intrusion of a new element among Islamic and Gnostic elements already present. That new element is paganism. As a matter of fact, the Nosairic Trinity compares with the pagan trinity of ancient Syria. To this they added mythological elements as well. Ali became the god of thunder; Husain's blood replaced the blood of Adonis, which accounted for the redness of the setting sun. Ritually, they included a curious mixture of Shi'ite and Christian Fêtes, and among them minor ones for the saints. The tombs of the saints, which were always on hilltops, were surrounded with trees, which were considered sacred. Nosairism, lost in its confused syncretism, was rejected by Orthodox Islam, but tolerated by Ismailism.

Meanwhile, Ismailism itself evolved to its final stages. Fifteen years after the mysterious disappearance of Caliph Hakem, the Fatimids once more assumed the title of Imam of Ismailians, in 1035. This Ismailian claim was established in Egypt as the official cult, and maintained itself until the Fatimid Dynasty was overthrown by Saladin, who in turn restored Orthodoxy, in the 12th century.

In the meantime, during the reign of the Fatimid Caliph, Mostansir, a Persian Ismailian called Hasan Ibn Sabbah came to Egypt as envoy of the Da'i of Iraq, in 1078. While he was there an event, analogous to the dispossession of Imam Ismail which had originally given rise to Ismailism, transpired. The

Caliph Mostansir dispossessed his heir, Nizar, in favour of his second son. Hasan Ibn Sabbah, prompted by political ambition, openly took Nizar's part, which led to his expulsion from Egypt; but he went to Syria, continued his propaganda in the Aleppo region, and, later, in Persia, where, with the help of his supporters he captured the Castle of Alamut in 1100. In a short time he had taken other castles, built new ones and reduced his followers to a blind submission. He added to his personal ascendancy by making his followers absorb a drug derived from Indian hemp—hashish. The name Assassin by which they were known is derived from it. The hashish evoked in them Paradisial hallucinations, and Hasan Ibn Sabbah made use of their state of mind to send them out to assassinate the princes and other great persons who opposed his power. Systematic assassinations had already been perpetrated in Islamic history by the Stranglers' sect,[1] in the 8th century, who had also interpreted the Koran allegorically.

Taking advantage of the disorders caused by the arrival of the Crusaders, Hasan was able to defy the Seljukid Sultans who were then masters of Western Asia, and establish an independent principality which maintained itself by terrorism under its first eight Grand-Masters, from 1090 to 1256.

The Fatimids had logically added to Ismailism a dictum which demanded passive obedience to the Imam. The Neo-Ismailism of Hasan, which was more of a secret political movement than a religious doctrine, gave it the force of law. Though the study of the Koran and its allegorical interpretation re-

[1] Encyclopedia of Islam, article Idjli.

mained, they meant nothing if the interpretation was not that of the Imam himself (Talim). This closed the door to all personal opinion. Hasan, though he declared himself the lieutenant of the Fatimid Imam, was nevertheless absolute master of the bodies as well as the consciences of his followers.

But one of Hasan's successors, the fourth Grand-Master of Alamut, went further, and broke the continuity of the doctrine by a sudden change which reminds one of that made by Hakem. While his predecessors had only called themselves the lieutenants of the Imam of Cairo, he declared himself to be the great-grandson of Nizar.[1] With this, he threw off all allegiance to the Fatimid Caliph, and declared himself the great Pontiff of Ismailism. The Grand-Master of Alamut had possession, at the time, not only of the fortified castles of Persia, but also of those of Syria, which had been gradually captured by his emissaries who had taken advantage of political disorders, and acquired the help of the Christians. "The Old Man of the Mountain," mentioned by the Western historians of the Crusades, is no other than the Syrian lieutenant of the Grand-Master of the Alamut. Half a century later, one of those lieutenants called Rashid-ed-Din Sinan repeated the procedure of Hasan Ibn Sabbah's adventure in Syria. He threw off his allegiance to Alamut and practiced the same mysterious political assassinations, thus obliging both the Crusaders and Saladin, who had overthrown the Fatimids in Egypt, to reckon with him.

In 1256, the Mongol invasion destroyed the

[1] The deposed son of the Fatimid Caliph Mostansir, whose rights were revindicated by Hasan Ibn Sabbah.

power of the Ismailians in Persia. As to those in Syria, they had already, a few years before, submitted to the Mamluks of Egypt, and lived in obscurity. Their descendants still live around ruins of fortified castles, and one finds them in feeble groups in Persia, in Central Asia, in Afghanistan, and in Zanzibar. In India, they have retained economic, if not political, power; and are known as the Khodja sect. Their present chief is Sir Muhammed Shah Ibn Agha Khan, better known as the Agha Khan, who is considered to be the 47th Imam by the Ismailians.

Hence, Ismailism, derived from Shi'ism, has had a powerful influence over the destinies of Islam through the political movements instigated by the Karmaths, Fatimids and Assassins. Moreover, it has had a part in the doctrinal evolution of Islamic thought, especially when it came into contact with Mutazelism, a movement which denied attributes to the Divinity, and accorded a prominent part to Reason. Before examining the Mutazelite doctrine, it would be well to summarise briefly Ismailian doctrine.

God has no attributes, and is above and beyond all conceptions; but, by His will, He has manifested Himself in the form of Universal Reason—the real divinity of the Ismailians. His only attribute is Science. Universal Reason has in turn created the Universal Soul, whose essential attribute is Life. This gave birth to Primal Matter, which passively takes on all the forms which Universal Reason gives to it. The Soul, for its part, struggles incessantly to acquire science, in order to rise to the level of Reason. To the interaction of these three principles are added those of Space and Time; and the action of all is directed upon Primal Matter. Therefore, beginning from God and ending with Primal Matter, there are seven principles. All these with the exception of God Himself, manifest themselves in the persons of the Prophets and the Imams, the seven cycles of whom we have already seen.[1]

Initiation into the Ismailian doctrine, founded upon the allegorical interpretation of the Koran, is in seven degrees. The majority of the initiated never rose above the second degree; the Da'i, that is, their missionaries, attained to the sixth degree. It was very rare for any Ismailian to be initiated as far as the seventh degree. Paradise was defined as the state of soul which reaches perfect knowledge; and Hell as the state of absolute ignorance. Further hell was considered to be temporary, and every soul, it was believed, came to earth by metempsychosis (Tanasukh) respectively, until such time as it had attained knowledge under the direction of the Imam. Evil would entirely disappear when the whole creation was, at last, assimilated by the Universal Reason.

The conception of Emanation is found with some modifications in a philosophical encyclopaedia composed by a group of Arab scholars known under the name of "Brothers of Purity." Further, the conception of cycles and their numerical symbolism reappeared with the Hurifi sect of Shi'ites. The Hurufi, meaning the interpreters of letters, were a sect founded in the 15th century, and their doctrine was adopted by the Bektashi Dervishes of the Ottoman Empire. Every cycle, according to their belief, was inaugurated by the apparition of one man, Adam,

[1] Page 194.

and came to an end with a Day of Judgment. The prophets were replaced by saints, who were considered as divine incarnations, and the first among them was the founder of the sect. Calculation based on the values attributed to the different letters of the alphabet played as great a part in their doctrine as in that of the Ismailians. The number seven retained all its importance.

Ismailism is not the only sect to contain ideas having some relation to Mutazelism. Nallino has noticed points of resemblance between the dogmas of the Kharidjite-Ibadites and of the Mutazelites, those of the latter being probably influenced by those of the former. It would be well to examine Mutazelism, which crystallised the rationalist tendencies so early evident in Syria. And parallel to these rationalistic tendencies, a mystical system also developed, at first in Iraq, having for its basis the eschatological visions of the Koran. From Rationalism came the philosophy of Islam, and its mysticism inspired works of edification and great poems.

THE PROBLEM OF FREE-WILL. Rationalism arises out of the problem of free will, and free-will was very obscurely, even contradictorily dealt with in the Koran. Is man entirely free in his actions, or is he absolutely dependent upon God? An appalling question, for it brings in its wake the question of divine justice. The exegetists of the Koran were forced to pose this question more from a legitimate desire to understand their religion than from an inclination to free-thinking.

Goldziher, in his examination of the Koran with respect to this question found it more contradictorily treated than any other subject. The power of Allah is absolute, no act of His can be questioned.[1] Allah is Just to every one. Nevertheless, "Allah will open the heart of him whom He intends to guide in the right path, and close the heart of him whom He intends to lead to err." [2] Further, it is said in the Koran "It is not for a soul to believe except by the permission of Allah." [3]

Opposed to these deterministic verses, there are others in the Koran which deal with free-will. "Judge between men with Justice, and do not *follow desire.*" [4] Again, "We showed them the right way, but they *chose error* above guidance.[5] *"Every one acts according to his manner."* [6] "Truth is from your Lord, so let him who pleases believe, and let him who pleases disbelieve." [7]

Goldziher also notices that in the verses where it is a question of sin, Allah does not lead men astray but allows the sinners to go astray (Adhalla). Like a lost traveller in the desert, man wanders forth into adventure. If he makes an effort to go right, Allah stretches out a helping hand and guides him; if he chooses the evil way, Allah leaves him in his error, but *it is not Allah* who has led him into evil. The conception of free-will may be clearly deduced from the following words: ". . . Even as they did not believe the first time, We will leave them in their error." [8] And again [9] Allah says: "They have forsaken

[1] Chap. 21:23.
[2] Chap. 6:126.
[3] Chap. 10:100.
[4] Chap. 38:26.
[5] Chap. 41:17.
[6] Chap. 17:86.
[7] Chap. 18:29.
[8] Chap. 6:111.
[9] Chap. 9:6.

Allah, so He has forsaken them." Thus Allah abandons those who forsake him, to their own devices.

The theologians of early Islam could not be expected to conceive so subtle an interpretation. According to Grimme, Muhammed himself evolved from a belief in free-will during his Meccan period a more and more categorical fatalism after the Hegira. It happened, rather, that as early as the end of the first century of the Hegira, this crude fatalism which made vice, virtue, reward and punishment independent of human will, disquieted the sense of justice of Muslems. It was in Syria that, for the first time, Muslem theologians, who were in contact with Christians, began to dispute this absolute fatalism. Fatalism in Arabic is Qadar, a technical term which is often followed by the word Qada. These two terms may be interpreted as follows: Qada is the universal and eternal decree of Allah; Qadar is the application of this decree in time. Good comes from Qada, while evil may accidentally come by Qadar.[1] As a result of the disputes on fatalism, two doctrines arose based on this interpretation of Qadar. The Qadarite doctrine, as it was called, restricted Qadar, that is, was against it being absolute and omnipotent. The Qadarites declared that Man himself created his own actions and consequently was responsible for his salvation or damnation. The partisans of the Djabarite doctrine, on the other hand, declared that the actions of man were, like those of inanimate nature, subject to divine constraint (Djabr).

Qadarism is therefore the earliest attempt to save Islam from the traditional conception of fatalism, not

[1] For secondary interpretations see the Encyclopedia of Islam, article Kadar.

from any urge towards free-thinking, but to satisfy purely the religious conscience. Naturally, the Omayyads condemned the new doctrine, for they availed themselves of the general belief in fatalism in order to keep their control over the people, and it was they who made their poets write: "Damnation is decreed from the beginning of time, in the eternal decrees of Allah." Omayyads had also a further reason to combat Qadarism, for it was the first Bid'a (innovation) to deal a blow at Orthodoxy.

A few years after the accession of the Abassids, and during the reigns of the Caliphs Mansur and Mamun, an external influence strongly affected Islam: Greek philosophy. The Nestorians translated the works of antiquity from the Syriac into the Arabic, first medical works, and then philosophic treatises. The importance of the work of those translators can never be exaggerated. They furnished the Arabs, a people whose genius was more lyrical than critical, with models of argumentation, of which the subtle Persian mind taught them to take full advantage. The resulting philosophy was, to tell the truth, a curious mixture proceeding mainly from Alexandria, under the influence of Hellenism: a combination of Aristotelianism, that is, a philosophy of reasoning based on experience, and of Platonic Idealism, which teemed with oriental visions. We will not attempt to give a sketch of this Muslem philosophy. Gaudefroy-Demombynes says: "The Arab philosophers, the depositaries of the science of their time, kept themselves on the extreme edge of Islam, though they always pretended to have respected all its principles."

Theologians then felt the danger of this philosophy to Orthodoxy, and learned to fight it with appropriate weapons—dialectics. And from this method of argumentation applied to theology the real philosophy of Islam came into being under the name of Kalem. Those who adhered to it were called the Mutakallimun. The oldest representatives of Kalem are the Mutazelites.

MUTAZELITES. The meaning of the word is "Those who isolate themselves," that is, the solitary ones. Mutazelism, as a matter of fact, seems to have been elaborated by ascetics, as a form of mysticism, but under Kalem it took more and more a rational tendency. The ascetic, Wasil Ibn Ata, who died in 748, and his principal companions were those who formulated its definite doctrine.

The great merit of the Mutazelites was to have made Aql, that is, reasoning, a criterion of religious knowledge. This principle led them to disentangle Monotheism from all the tradition and popular elements which had encumbered it. In brief, they intended to restrict themselves to the notions of justice and divine unity.

They believed even more than did the Qadarist: that man is responsible for his own actions without the intervention of Allah. But this concept of free-will in man logically set a limit to the omnipotence of God as conceived by the Orthodox. The moment man is acknowledged to have free choice in his actions the Divinity finds itself under the obligation of rewarding those who are good, and punishing those who are evil; and this follows not from the free-will and omnipotence of God but as a necessary act of grace. In other words, for the absolute and arbitrary power of Allah, the Mutazelites substituted the duty of Allah towards His creatures: man is free, but God is not.

What was Good and what was Evil? The Orthodox said: "Good is that which Allah ordains: evil is that which He forbids." But the Mutazelites declared that there were an absolute Good and Evil which were determined not by Allah, but by Reason.

So much for the concept of divine justice. As for the concept of Divine Unity, the Mutazelites reacted vigorously against the exaggerated anthropomorphism of some of the Orthodox doctors. The latter had attributed a body to Allah; but the Mutazelites considered Allah to be Pure Spirit, and consequently they rejected all those attributes which, in their opinion, led to Polytheism, and belittled the nature of Allah. The Orthodox objected in vain to this negation of the attributes of God, saying that it was equivalent to putting aside the very idea of God (Tatil). Further, even the Koran speaks of attributes, said the Orthodox; which fact could not be denied.

This question of the attributes of Allah led to a discussion of the Koran itself. Could Allah have the attribute of speech? According to the Orthodox, the Word is an eternal attribute of God, and not created; therefore the Koran is the manifestation of the Divine Word, and not created. The answer of the Mutazelites to this argument was: Muhammed did not hear the voice of God, but the voice of an organ created by Him. Consequently, the Koran, being the word of Him who spoke to Muhammed, must also necessarily be created; otherwise it would be eternal the same as Allah. Certain Mutazelites went as far as to claim that human genius could surpass the perfection of the Koran.

In brief, their doctrine comprised three fundamental ideas: (1) Man is free; (2) Man can distinguish in Allah attributes of substance and attributes of fact; (3) The Koran is not eternal.

The idea of the Koran being created was adopted with enthusiasm by the Abassid Caliph Mamun, who imposed it as an article of faith, in 833. The dissentients, among whom was Ibn Hanbal, were subject to an often fanatical inquisition, which lasted for half a century, and which brought about a complete confusion among the believers. Mutazelism, which had begun in liberalism, ended in intolerance. But Mutawakil, the third successor of Mamun, deeming it necessary to strengthen his political and religious power, turned for help to the Turkish mercenaries who were new converts, and to the Orthodox theologians. From 847 onwards, he reacted against both Mutazelism and Mysticism; but Mutazelism remained as menacing as ever, and the quarrels between the Rational Mutazelites and the Orthodox traditionalists continued to divide Islam.

ASHARISM. The reconciliation between Mutazelism and Orthodoxy was realised in the 10th century by a Mutazelite, Ashari, who at the age of forty returned to Orthodoxy and reformed it. To be exact, his doctrine was more in the nature of an arrangement than a reconciliation. He rejected both the excessive rationalism of the Mutazelites and the excessive formalism of the Orthodox. He steered a middle course between the Mutazelites who had rejected all the divine attributes, and the traditionalists (Hashwiya, ahl-al-hadith) who believed only in the letter of the Koran, and attributed human organs to God. While the sect of the Djamites professed the belief that man had no power over his actions and therefore no responsibility, Ashari declared man responsible for his actions. While the Mutazelites considered the Koran to be created as against the traditionalists who declared it to be eternal (including the material with which it was written, and the material on which it was written), Ashari accepted the Koran as the eternal word of God, but declared the lettering composing it and the ink and materials with which it was composed as being of human production.

With respect to the processes of reasoning, it was impossible for Ashari to eliminate reason (Aql), which had been established by the Mutazelites as being the chief faculty to provide the data of religious knowledge; but he limited the applicability of Nazar, that is, the speculative knowledge of man with regard to God. On the other hand, he condemned the Taqlid of the Orthodox, that is, the acceptance as authority of words and acts without discussing the underlying motives. In brief, Ashari defended Orthodoxy with the weapons he borrowed from its enemies, a procedure which was pleasing to nobody. His doctrine was completed by his disciples, the most remarkable among whom was Baqillani, who added some metaphysical concepts; but according to Goldziher, a century had to pass before "he was welcomed as the greatest authority on the dogma of Orthodox Islam," and this was due to Nizam-ul-Mulk, the famous prime minister of the Seljukids, who supported Asharism without declaring Mutazelites to be heretics.[1]

THE MYSTICS. At the end of the same century

[1] See page 229.

many of the mystical ideas dispersed throughout Islam were also reconciled to Orthodoxy by a great man: Ghazali. While the Rationalists believed that truth could be reached only by the faculty of reason, the Mystics affirmed that it could be perceived by the faculty of intuition. In this domain, Ghazali played the same part as Ashari had done in the domain of scholasticism. In the very early days of Islam, ascetic practices had appeared, undoubtedly due to the influence of the Christians, some of whom bound themselves to columns, others lived in fetters, and some went on pilgrimages on foot, under a vow of silence.

Nevertheless such practices had already been suggested by certain verses in the Koran.[1] A series of relevant passages are found in Massignon's "Essai" on page viii, and their tendency was strengthened by the eschatological vision of the Koran. But any concern with matters of that sort was put aside during the period of conquest when minds were occupied with worldly gains. Further, there existed sayings condemning asceticism which were attributed to Muhammed; though in life he had showed a great respect to Muslems who devoted themselves to prayer and fasting, without himself or his companions being ascetics in the strict sense of the word.

Ascetic tendencies asserted themselves in Iraq by way of reaction against the luxurious habits introduced by the Caliph Othman and developed later

[1] "Allah is the light of the heavens and the earth" (Chap. 24:35). "He is the first and the last, and the outward and the inward" (Chap. 57:3). "... Everything is perishable except His Face" (Chap. 28:88). "Verily We have created man and We know what his soul suggests to him for We are nigher to him than his life-blood" (Chap. 50:16). These are among the passages which gave birth to Muslem Mysticism.

under the Omayyads. This led to innovations of which Goldziher notes two: A liturgy replacing the five daily canonical prayers by mystical litanies; and an ethic substituting an absolute passive quietism which led to almost complete indifference to the external world for the confidence of the Orthodox in God (Tawwakul).

A little later the Mystics adopted the woollen mantle, the Suf; from which their name, Sufi, was derived. According to Massignon's article in the Encyclopaedia of Islam, entitled, Tasawwuf, the first groups of Sufis organised in Kufa in the 7th and the 8th centuries and in Basra in the 8th century. Bagdad became the centre of the movement in the second half of the 9th century.

These Muslem Mystics, like any other Mystics, sought in solitude a state of ecstasy which could be reached through a series of initiating experiences, the culmination being complete union with the Supreme Being.

Asceticism hitherto had lacked a doctrinal basis, found it in the doctrines of Neo-Platonism, which were widely disseminated in the 9th century. Ghazali speaks of Sufism as in the eleventh century "consisting of sentiments rather than definitions." This goes to prove how divers were the definitions contributed to Sufism by Muslems.

There is no reason to believe Muslem Mysticism to be of alien origin. It arose spontaneously on Muslem soil, though one can trace Christian, Iranian and even Hindu (Vedanta) influences. But among all these influences, the most marked are the Greek, especially among the late Mystics, who enriched their technical vocabulary from that source. Further, the

Platonic doctrine of Emanation led the Muslem Mystics to define their feelings; to them the world was a mirror in which the Divine Being was reflected, therefore, its existence was only in appearance, and to reach reality one must escape from this appearance, be released from one's personal life and become one with the Divine, which alone was real. This conception was called Fana, and was a logical development from Shath. The word used to describe the ecstatic states of certain of the early Mystics.

Ibn Sab'in of Murcia defined the mystical tendencies of the Arab philosophers of the 13th century as follows: "While the Ancient Philosophers wanted to resemble God, the Mystics wanted to be absorbed in God." Sufism, therefore, in the 17th century was derived from asceticism, and ended in Monism. Ibn Arabi, one of the greatest theoreticians of Sufism, formulated this Monism. A later author, Ibn Taimiya[1] summarised his doctrine in the following sentence: "The existence of created things is nothing but the existence of the Creator; everything springs from the divine essence and finally returns to it." This dominating idea of Sufism gave birth to several great poems; for instance, the Masnavi of Djalalu'ddin Rumi.

Though it may seem as if the Mystics had nothing in common with other Muslems, nevertheless they remained attached to Islam and interpreted verses of the Koran to support their ideas; just as the most advanced Shi'ites had done by interpreting the Koran allegorically. The Mystics had another point of contact with Shi'ism. They venerated Ali as the

[1] See page 252.

founder of the mystical tradition. On the other hand, the Shi'ites rejected the Sufis.

From the 7th century onwards Mystics gathered together in convents, called Khanagrah or Tekke in the Orient, and Zawiya in the West. There were convents even for women in Syria and in Egypt, in the 13th and the 14th centuries.

These convents, at first a refuge for some small group, gradually transformed themselves into schools of holiness, where novices followed the teachings of a spiritual guide, and attained to the "right way." Though these mystical teachings varied in detail, fundamentally they remained the same. From the 12th century onward their activities became political as well as religious, particularly in North Africa. The oldest religious order worthy of the name was that of Qadiriya, founded by Abdul-Qadir-Gaylani in the 12th century. Others followed in succession: Rifaiya; Mawlawiya (the dancing dervishes); Shadiliya (African); Badawiya (Egyptian). A list of these orders will be found in Massignon's article entitled Tarika, in the Encyclopaedia of Islam.

The rules of these Orders varied, but they all had one rite in common: the repetition of dhikr, litanies of Allah in a loud voice, or mentally sometimes accompanied by gestures. The practice of dhikr is based on a Koranic verse.[1] This brought in the use of the chaplet (Subha) consisting of a hundred beads,[2] which corresponded to the hundred attributes of Allah. It may have been imported from India; but, anyway, its use became general in the 15th century. The formulas of dhikr vary with the order which

[1] Chap. 33:41.

[2] Ninety-nine beads among the Hanifite Sunnites.

recites them; and as an aid to reaching ecstatic states music and dancing are sometimes added; for instance by the Mawlawiya. The Isawiya (or Aissaua) go further and introduce barbaric practices based on animism, which are in complete opposition to Orthodoxy.

It must be understood that these Orders included vast religious organisations as well as small local brotherhoods. Further, they differed in character. In some of these brotherhoods, especially in Morocco, the religious element was secondary; for instance, with those of the Shooters and the Jugglers, both of Morocco.

In every case the order was governed by a Grand-Master, known as the Sheikh or Pir, who authorised representatives to rule over the affiliated convents of the same Order. They all lived on donations made in cash or in kind. The Grand-Master enjoyed absolute authority over the brothers of his Order, who were as inert in his hands "as the corpse in the hands of one who washes the dead" (Perinda ac Cadavar). The Grand-Master had the mysterious gift of spiritual power (Baraka), and it passed from one Grand-Master to another. The founder of the Order from whom this spiritual power originally came was venerated as a saint.

The cult of Saints, both men and women, was among the greatest of the innovations in Islam.[1] Though entirely opposed to Monotheism, this cult spread rapidly in Islam, particularly among the Berbers, owing to the influence of Sufism. Bel says:

[1] A saint is called Wali in the East, and Marabut in Maghreb; where the tomb is also called Marabut, whether it is an actual sepulchre or a pile of stones.

"In no other Muslem country has the cult of Saints been carried so far. One can say without hesitation that among the peasants and women, this saint-cult, accompanied by animistic and naturist rites, constituted the only religion."

As in other religions, the saint-cult sometimes supplanted the worship of God. As a matter of fact, in the eyes of the masses, always willing to believe in miracles, the saints appeared as more accessible than the majestic and far-off God of Islam. The lives of the saints were full of miraculous doings, some of which were not always worthy of the Golden Legend. Further, the cult of a local saint, which at times eliminated the need for a pilgrimage to Mecca, often had some past cult as its origin. For instance, the cult of Sheikh Mashuk (Beloved) had behind it the cult of Adonis. One finds everywhere traces of this cult; on stones, trees and animals. In the Fête of Tantat in Egypt, dedicated to the serpent of the mountain of Sheikh Haridi, a donkey had a sacred significance. Some of these saints, even in their lifetime, were honoured as such, particularly in Maghreb, though they over-rode and, indeed, despised all social conventions. The Dervishes of the Malamatiya are compared to the Cynics of antiquity, because of their complete contempt of social propriety.

It was precisely this contempt, though of a less definite order, and their indifference to canonical practices which made the Sufis appear suspicious in the eyes of the Orthodox, long before the Monism of the 13th century Mystics. Nevertheless, if Orthodoxy acted rigorously against certain advanced Mystics, among whom Halladj [1] was the most famous, it was always tolerant towards the more moderate Sufis. However, the rigorists reproached the Sufis for their preference for meditation instead of prayer, and for their negligence of the religious practices of the Sunnites. As a matter of fact, Sufism broadened the religious outlook which had been restricted by Kalem, but they unconsciously retarded theological science by insisting so much on intuition. The adepts of Sufism would have nothing but a religion of the heart.

Among the several attempts made at reconciliation between Orthodoxy and Sufism was that of Ghazali, who died in 1111. He was one of the greatest spirits of Islam, and it was he who undertook to establish the just mean between the theologians and the Sufis; that is, to use his words: "Between those who call themselves the disciples of Reason and speculation, and those who consider themselves the elect of God, gifted with intuition and possessing knowledge of the truth through ecstasy." On one hand were the Scholastics, who by giving to Allah attributes entirely different from human attributes, isolated Him from His creation to such an extent that one could ask whether He had any actual power over it; and on the other hand were the Mystics who, admitting a

[1] Halladj was crucified in Bagdad in 922 for his extreme mystical opinions. Before ascending the cross, he prayed for the people who had gathered to see his martyrdom. Some of his prayer is considered very beautiful, and often quoted: "And these Thy servants who are gathered to slay me, in zeal for Thy religion and in desire to win Thy favour, forgive them O Lord, and have mercy upon them; for verily if Thou hadst revealed to them that which Thou hast revealed to me, they would not have done what they have done. . . ."

gradual fusion of the world with Allah, were logically led to affirm that Allah was All.

Ghazali rejected casuistry and its abuses, whether it was that of Kalem, of Philosophy, or of Fiqh. He says:

"There is a class of men who restrict their thinking to the science of judicial consultation. . . . They call their knowledge—which leads them to Jurisprudence—Ilm-al-Fiqh and Ilm-al-Madhab, and they imagine that it is the same as the science of religion. They neglect the study of the Book of God and the Sunna of the Prophet. When one questions a jurist about those things the omission of which leads to eternal damnation, he knows not what to answer. On the other hand, he can quote volumes on the subtleties of casuists. . . . One should consider a man mad if he studies such things with the aim of approaching God."

According to Ghazali, the real science of religion is "the love of the heart for the Divine, the inner prayer, these being the means by which the human conscience possesses to approach God." Therefore detailed discussions, and theological or judicial subtleties, must be replaced by the love of God, Who has created the intuitive life of the soul.

Thus Ghazali introduced mystical love into Orthodoxy. But from Sufism he banished two extreme elements: indifference to religious practices, and the Pantheistic ideal. The latter he limited without destroying it. In brief, he brought wisdom into Sufism, and life into Orthodoxy. According to Macdonald, Ghazali made use of reason to destroy reason, by proving its inability to lead to absolute knowledge;

and he made use of tradition to discipline, to guide and to curb the imagination of the Mystics.

Ghazali really regenerated Islam by achieving in his works, a synthesis of the traditional, rational and mystical elements. Furthermore, one proof of his rapid and profound influence, comparable to that of Thomas Aquinas, is the discredit into which Aristotelianism fell in the East. After this, Arab Philosophy emigrated to Spain, where it shed its supreme light in the 12th century. It is well known how the scientific works of Greece, studied and criticised by Arabs, translated into Hebrew by Jews of Spain and Southern France, then translated into Latin, penetrated Europe. Thus Islam took its place in the chain which links ancient thought with modern thought, and played a considerable part in the history of civilisation.

Meanwhile, the great sectarian movements spent their last energy in the 13th century. Conflicts between Orthodoxy and Liberalism, between philosophy and mysticism were appeased. The rivalries between Sunnism and Shi'ism were to be henceforth more political than religious. Two more movements were to manifest themselves later, one in the 18th century, under the name of Wahhabism; and the other in the 19th century, under the name of Babism. The fundamental aims of these two movements were, respectively, to restore Islam to its primitive simplicity, and to bring new elements into Islam.

CHAPTER VI

The Turkish and Persian Hegemony

THE history of Islam like the history of Christianity records great invasions of Barbaroi, that is, strangers. The Barbarian invaders of the Christian world in the 5th century were progressively absorbed by the Christian Church, which was then the only power strong enough to assimilate them among the ruins of the Roman Empire. The invasions of the Arab Muslem Empire in the eleventh century were of a different nature. The invaders came themselves with the purpose of establishing the religious and political unity of the Muslem Empire. Some came from the extreme West, for instance the Sunnite Berbers who came to oppose the Hillalian invasions, and were emissaries from the Shi'ite Caliph in Cairo sent to stop Christian progress in Spain. These invaders from the extreme West were the Almoravids and the Almohads. The other invaders came from Central Asia, and were the opposition of the Sunnite Turks to Iranian Shi'ism; hence both could justify their conquests as being wars based on religious principles.

THE BERBERS IN NORTH AFRICA

THE ALMORAVIDS. They belonged mainly to the Lamtuna, a subdivision of the great Berber tribe of the Sanhadja. The part they played among the

Berbers has already been mentioned. The Lamtunas were related to the Tuaregs, and like them were veiled. They led a nomadic life, wandering across the territories situated south of Morocco towards Nigeria and extending to the Tripolitan region of the desert, where they fought the Sudanese. The Sudanese Kingdoms had always been in relation with North Africa; and Christianity had penetrated into some regions, especially in Nubia, and perhaps as far as Songhoy in Nigeria. The rest of the country was still dominated by pagan animism.

In the 11th century the Ghana Empire flourished in western Sudan on the confines of the deserts. Its rulers were black princes whose suzerainty extended over the Berber tribes of the Sahara, including the Lamtunas. It happened that about this period one of the Lamtuna chiefs was in search of a theologian capable of teaching clearly the doctrines of Islam. After a vain search in Kairuan, he found his man in Morocco, in the person of Ibn Yasin. This man after gathering around him some of the Lamtuna, established himself in Senegal in a military monastery known under the name of Ribat.[1] Ibn Yasin, as head of the monastery, exacted a passive obedience from his followers, and established absolute equality between the members of his Order. His aim was clear: to restore Orthodoxy, in the form of the Malekite Rite, among the Muslems of Maghreb. Towards 1042, he began to preach Islam to the Berbers of the Sahara and to the Negroes of Takrur.

1 The name al-morabit is derived from Ribat, meaning those of Ribat, and it eventually became Almoravid. The word Ribat is the same as the name of the city Rabat and is found in the word Marabut. The Ribat, which were Islamic monasteries, are reminiscent of those of the Knights Templars of the Crusades.

These last wanting to escape from the yoke of the pagan princes of Ghana, willingly embraced Islam. Thus an army of faith came into existence, and was soon on the offensive. The fall of Ghana, in 1076 on the one hand, opened the way for the Islamisation of the Sudan, a process which after several setbacks reached its zenith in the 18th and the 19th centuries; while, on the other hand, the Sanhadja-Lamtuna marched into Morocco, where they encountered their age-old enemies, the Berbers of Zeoata. They captured Sidjilmasa on the march, and Ibn Yasin perished in the Holy War; but in Ibn Tashfina was found a worthy successor who founded Marakesh and made it his capital. Thus Morocco was once more taken out of the hands of the heretical Berbers. Ibn Tshfina marched East, and in 1082 was master of the territory from Morocco to Algiers, that marking the eastern boundary of his conquests. He erected mosques throughout the country, tangible signs of the ideas which dominated the Almoravid mentality, a fervent movement which later was to provoke the Crusades, and which had begun among the Muslems of Africa. As a matter of fact, it was this religious zeal for the defence of Islam which led Ibn Tashfina to listen to the Muslem kings of Spain when they implored his help. The Caliphate of Cordova was then upheld by Arabs and Berbers whose dissensions had divided Muslem Spain into small kingdoms. This internal division had naturally facilitated the task of the Christian princes who wanted to reconquer Spain. Ibn Tashfina, after a series of four campaigns, defeated the Christian princes, among whom was the Cid, and paralysed their power. He also subdued the native Muslem princes who had asked for help, and reconstituted an Empire which at his death included Muslem Spain as well as the major portion of North Africa. But the influence of the decadent and refined civilisation of Andalusia proved too much for the sturdy monk-warriors. The son of Ibn Tashfina, born of a Christian mother, was bred amid Spanish culture, and was a delicate man of letters, who, when he succeeded to that rigid puritan his father, brought North Africa under the direct influence of Spanish civilisation for some years.

THE ALMOHADS. The decline of the Almoravids, which continued for a century, began with the death of Tashfina. During his son's reign, another rigid puritan emerged though this time not from the nomadic, but from the sedentary tribes of the High-Atlas of Morocco who were known as the Berbers of Masmuda. The new chief was Ibn Tumart, his name being a Berber diminutive of the Arab name Omar, and he was superior in capacity to Ibn Tashfina. Ibn Tashfina had merely been a theologian, but Ibn Tumart imitated the Fatimid Caliph Obaid-Allah by proclaiming himself Mahdi. Ibn Tashfina's ideas were based on a strict observance of the Malekite Rite, as understood by an exclusive study of the Law from the works of the Doctors of the Law.[1] Tumart had his own conception of faith which he opposed to this. His was founded primarily on the Koran, and then on the traditions and principles of the Law. In brief, he went back to the religious sources of the law; but, further, he condemned the literal interpretation of the Koran, as adopted by the Almoravids. As a rigorous Asharite,[2]

[1] See the passage on Ghazali on page 215.
[2] See page 207.

he accused the Almoravids of not believing in a purely divine unity. His own creed was based on an absolute belief in Tawhid, that is the unity of God. The word Tawhid gave rise to the word Muwwahid, which finally became Almohad, which means "those who believe in divine unity." According to the Almohads, the Almoravids gave human attributes to Allah, and considered the Koran as having been created throughout all eternity; therefore they were anthropomorphists, and guilty of Polytheism (Shirk), and must be fought as if they were infidels. We will see later how the Wahhabites made use of this idea in their ferocious monotheism.

Ibn Tumart, in his writing and preaching, did not use only Arabic, the language of the theologians. Just as Luther abandoned Latin for German, so he abandoned Arabic for the dialect of the Mountain Berbers, in order to make his doctrines comprehensible to them—this fact alone was enough to give him originality. On his return from the Orient he brought to Maghreb which had become sterilised by the narrow formalism of the Malekite Rite, a theological culture vitalised by Ghazali. But his reforming ardour scandalised his world, and being expelled in succession from Bugiz, Tlemsen and Marakesh, he took refuge among his tribe in the High-Atlas, from where he could contemplate the Almoravid capital. He evangelised his tribe, and after receiving the allegiance of the regional Berber tribes, declared himself Mahdi, and began to preach the Holy War. Thus, in 1121, the Empire of the Almohads came into existence.

The serious import of this movement was that Ibn Tumart, by declaring himself Mahdi, had not only risen against the Malekite Almoravids, but against Orthodox Islam as well; for as Mahdi he denied the right given by the Orthodox to the Mudjtahids (doctors of law) to interpret the Law according to personal opinion. This right to personal interpretation, Ibn Tumart granted to the Imam only; thus showing how near he approached to Shi'ism.[1] The infallible Imam, the chief of the community, was naturally the Mahdi,—that is to say; Ibn Tumart himself.

Ibn Tumart, obsessed by the example of the Prophet, appears to have been more a man of inspiration than a man of action. The person who was to realise his ideas was Abd-al-Momin, a man of Tlemsen, who became to Ibn Tumart, what Omar had been to the Prophet. The Berbers of Atlas refused to pay taxes to the Almoravids, and attacked the troops which were sent to punish them. At first the hostilities were unfavourable to the Almohads; but, after Ibn Tumart's death, Abd-al-Momin descended from the mountains with his followers, and after a few years of defensive war passed to the offensive, capturing Tlemsen, Fas and Merakesh in 1147. Further, he took advantage of the rising against the Almoravids in Spain to establish his authority there also. Abd-al-Momin's conquest of North Africa was facilitated by the civil war between the Hammadids of Bugiz and the Zirids of Kairuan, as well as by the decisive attacks of the Sicilian Normans on the Zirids. From the Atlantic to Tripoli the country was for the first time under a single master who appointed governors, and established a cadastral organisation which had been hitherto non-existent in those

1 See page 198.

lands. A little before his death in 1163, Abd-al-Momin declared himself Caliph, bringing the number of Caliphs in Islam up to three; the other two being respectively in Bagdad and Cairo. His claim was accepted by the companions of Ibn-Tumart, the Mahdi, and his dynastic rights established. His descendants continued to reign until 1269, when Merakesh was captured by the Merinids. Until the year 1236, they reigned over the whole of the Empire founded by Abd-al-Momin, erecting monuments and patronising the Arab philosophers of Spain.[1] But they were being continually obliged to give way to the influence of the companions of Mahdi, which undermined their authority; and they had to sustain a hard fight against two descendants of the Almoravids, which weakened them still more. Then their brilliant victory at Alarcos in Spain against the Christians was annulled a few years later by the disaster of Las Navas. Attacked both in Africa and in Spain, the dynasty was rapidly exhausted. The provinces tried to break away from the Empire, and there were revolutions, all of which finally forced the Almohads to give autonomy to governors, who in turn declared their complete independence.

DIVISIONS. From the ruins of the Almohad Empire three new dynasties emerged: the Hafsids in Tunis; the Abd-al-Wadits in Tlemsen; and the Merinids in Fas. History repeats itself. These three kingdoms were the offspring of three other African kingdoms of the 9th century: the Aghlabids, the Rustamids, and the Idrissids. As for Muslem Spain, the progress of the Christian Reconquista had reduced it to the small kingdom of Granada where the Nas-

[1] See page 217.

rids, creatures of the palace of Alhambra, were in power. Marçais speaks of them as "crystallising all the elegance and fantasy of the Muslem art of Spain." The Nasrids held their own against the Christians and the Merinids by a policy of balance until 1492. It was in this same year that Ferdinand and Isabella were to expel the last Arab Prince. A few months later Christopher Columbus was to plant their standard on the soil of the New World.

Of these three African kingdoms, the first attempts to establish dynasties in Tunis, Algeria and Morocco, that of the Merinids was the strongest. It resembled the Almoravids in its general traits; its policy was that of the Almohads: defense of Spain and extension towards East Africa. But the Merinids were also exhausted in this double struggle. The rivalries of these three kingdoms occupy the end of the 14th and the beginning of the 15th centuries. By the middle of the 14th century the Merinids had recoiled back to their early boundaries in Morocco where the Portuguese were acquiring a foothold. The wheels of fortune had turned: it was now the Christians who crossed the sea and threatened Africa, whose coasts were to be henceforth infested by barbaric corsairs. In the 16th century Islam strove against the attacks of the Christians in both a religious and a military sense. Religion in fact dominated this part of their history. The Almoravids and the Almohads were champions of faith. As for the Merinids, though less zealous, they favoured the cult of saints, and mystical trends in general, tendencies which contributed towards a religious revival, and helped to break the Christian offensive in the 16th century.

The Turks in Asia

The peoples of Central Asia oscillated in their attack between China and Persia according to the powers of resistance of each. From the 8th to the 10th century, China, divided by internal dissensions, could not resist attack; but in the second half of the 10th century the accession of the Sung Dynasty inaugurated an era of regeneration. The nomads of Central Asia, always in need of good pastures which their steppes and deserts could not provide, and obliged to migrate to more fertile lands, then turned their incursions towards the West, as the weakening of the Caliphate in Bagdad made that quarter more easily accessible.

We have already seen in the second chapter how the eastern and the western boundaries of the Abassid Caliphate had been receding. Everywhere separatist tendencies were apparent. Both Armenia and Arabia had broken away from the Empire. The Caliph's domain was now restricted to Iraq, where the Shi'ite Buids were the rulers in fact. Yet the Faineant Caliph, though entirely under the tutelage of the "Maires du Palais," was still the seat of all authority, at least, in the eyes of theoreticians. Meanwhile, another Caliphate had been established in Spain, and still another heretical Caliphate maintained itself in Cairo. Nevertheless it was to the Caliph in Bagdad that several great princes turned for their investiture: Mahmud, the Ghaznavid, had solicited official recognition from the Caliph of Bagdad, who had the title of Amir-al-Muminin (Commander of the Believers); and, a century later, that is, in 1175, Saladin, the incontestable master of Syria and Egypt, also asked for his investiture of the Abassid Caliph, the last phantom.

Meanwhile, from the eleventh century onwards three invasions were to take place in Muslem Asia: that of the Seljukids; of the Mongols; and of the armies of Timur. Did the invaders and the invaded influence each other reciprocally?

THE SELJUKIDS. In the tenth century the Turks of Central Asia were divided into three principal groups: Ouigurs, residing in the mountain regions of Tian Chan; Karluks, in Eastern Turkestan (Kashgar); and Ghozz or Oghuz, on the borders of Transoxiana. The Karluks were converted to Islam in the 10th century, and spread along the Syr-Daria (Yaxarte), from where they drove the Oghuz Turks to the south and east. The Oghuz Turks separated into two sections, one of which invaded Russia and marched on Greece, where they were exterminated; and the other of which being at the same time the greater in number embraced Islam, and invaded Transoxiana under the Seljuk Princes. From 1035 onwards, the grandsons of Seljuk, the founder of the Dynasty, attacked Khorasan, which then belonged to the Ghaznevids, and conquered it after a war of five years. This event was of great consequence as it laid open Iran and, through it, the Islamic lands to the peoples of Central Asia. Two years later, after subduing Persia, the Seljukids carried their Holy War into Christian lands, traversing Anatolia and ravaging Armenia. This was the revenge of Islam for the victorious offensive of the Byzantine Emperors of the 10th century. In 1055, Togrul entered Bagdad, put an end to Persian influence and the domination of the Shi'ite Buids, and had himself recognised as sovereign by the Caliph, whose daughter he had married—a far-off sign of the coming Ottoman Caliphate.

Taking advantage of the internal disorders of the Empire, the Seljukids continued their incursions into Byzantium for about ten years, until the defeat of the Emperor Romanus Diogenes delivered Asia Minor into their hands. Meanwhile, they invaded Syria and Palestine, where they were brought face to face with the Fatimids, hence the age-old conflict between Orthodoxy and Shi'ism was re-opened. The power of the Fatimids was on the decline, the Caliph in Cairo being like the one in Bagdad, a puppet in the hands of his mercenaries who were composed of Turks, Berbers and Negroes, the races whose rivalries had exhausted the Empire. Hence while the Seljukids were busy conquering Jerusalem in 1070, the Eygptians were suffering from revolutions and famine, and their precious library collected by the Fatimids was being destroyed. A general of Armenian origin restored order in Egypt, for a time, but his struggles to keep away the Seljukids from Palestine and Syria were in vain. The Seljukids' desire to attack Egypt was, after all, quite logical, since the Fatimids were the last stronghold of Shi'ism. It was then that France, frightened at this expansion which menaced both Byzantium and the Holy Places, decided on a Crusade.

It was in this way that the Seljukids became, for a time, the champions of Orthodox Islam against Christian invasions, until they were able to establish a political unity in Asia, but they were to establish a religious unity as well, by reducing Shi'ite influence and neutralising the occult power of the Assassin sect.[1] They owed their rapid victory to a military and administrative organisation of a high order, which contrasted strongly with the anarchy of their enemies. This organisation was due to three great Seljuk Sultans, and to a minister of Persian origin, known as Nizam-ul-Mulk. He protected Ghazali, and his power makes one think of the Barmecides of Bagdad. Nizam-ul-Mulk left a "Treaty of Government," in which he revealed his methods of administration. The work is translated by Shefer. The greatest of the Seljukid rulers, Malik-Shah, appears to have been Persian in taste, though a Turk by race. There were now two Islamised Turkish peoples: one, very conservative and under Chinese influence, remained in Turkestan; the other in Western Asia, was profoundly changed by the Byzantine, Arab and Persian civilisations, and at the moment when the latter was at its strongest. But this cultural transformation did not affect the rigid orthodoxy of the Seljukids themselves. Nizam-ul-Mulk speaks of the Seljuk Sultan in this way: "The Sultan insists on seeing every work that deals with religion and the obligations which religion imposes. . . . Once or twice a week he receives in audience the doctors of the Law."

At Malik-Shah's death in 1092, his empire, too vast to fall to one man, was divided between his brothers and his sons. One of these took Persia, the other Syria, and another Anatolia. The dissension which arose between the Seljukid princes helped the Crusaders; and while Malik-Shah's sons were quarrelling in Persia, the Crusading army inflicted two decisive defeats on the Anatolian Seljukids, that of

[1] See page 196.

Dorylee in 1097, and Antioch in 1098. This was a fatal blow to the power of the Seljukids, and from the 12th century onwards their empire was divided into small principalities, resembling the division of the Spanish Caliphate a century earlier. The authority of the Seljukid state which was essentially military was now delegated to provincial governors whose power was increased as the central power declined, a state of affairs similar to that which had led to the rise of Saffarid and Samanid Dynasties in Oriental Persia. These Seljukid Governors who had become independent are known in history as Ata-Begs,[1] and became the founders of local dynasties ruling in Syria, Mesopotamia, Armenia and Persia. Thus dismembered, the empire exposed itself to the depredations of outside powers.

At this time the people of Turkestan appeared on the scene. Sandjar, the third son of Malik-Shah, the cultivated and heroic prince, defended Eastern Persia against them on the same frontier which had been defended by Sasanids and Samanids in the old days; but it was then an Iranian people defending themselves against Turanians. Now it was a Turanian who was defending Persia against a people of his own race. The forces against him were the Kara-Khitais, who were peoples from North China who camped in the Oriental Turkestan; the Oghuz Turks of the Kirghiz steppes; and the princes of Kharzem and Khiva, known as the Khorasmin to the Crusaders. These last were the descendants of a former slave of Malik-Shah, whom he had appointed governor to Khiva. Sandjar, the last of the great Sel-

[1] Ata means father; Beg means prince. The name was formerly used as a title for tutors of princes.

jukids, put up a desperate resistance for thirty years until his death in 1157; but he was not able to prevent the Kara-Khitais and Kharzems from dividing Transoxiana between themselves.

At the end of the 12th century, Seljukid Persia, torn with revolutions, was captured by the Kharzemians, and fifteen years later they conquered Otrar, the capital of Kara-Khitai, whose power they had already destroyed. It was now the turn of Ghazna, the capital of the Ghorid Dynasty, which had replaced the Ghaznevids both in Afghanistan and in Hindustan. Thus a new empire, that of the Kharzemians, restored the political unity of Western Asia which had been divided into small units by Ata-Begs. But the Kharzemians were not able to restore Asia's religious unity. The impeccable orthodoxy of the Seljukids was replaced by the Shi'ism of the Kharzemians in 1228. They were contemplating the destruction of even the Abassid Caliphate, but the Mongol invasion did not give them the time.

Nevertheless, if Shi'ism was regaining a preponderance in Asia, however momentarily, it was losing its hold in Egypt. In 1171, Saladin, a Turk, the son of an officer of the Ata-Begs, taking advantage of the decline of Fatimids, which had been hastened by the discords among their vezirs and by the attacks of Crusaders, had re-established Orthodoxy in Egypt. The Eyubid Dynasty founded by Saladin,[1] reorganised Egypt. Thus this great Sunnite State extended its frontiers down to the Euphrates, suppressed several dynasties of Ata-Begs and assumed the rôle of champion of Orthodox Islam in succession to the Seljukids. With this, the centre of the Islamic strug-

[1] Named after Saladin's grandfather: Eyub.

gle against the onslaught of the Crusades was transported to Egypt and Syria. The defeats inflicted on the Christian armies by Saladin in Syria would have been fatal to the Crusades if Saladin's heirs had not started to quarrel among themselves. It was a repetition of the dissensions of the Seljukid Princes. This internal disunion in the Eyubid state naturally exposed it to outside attacks, and the Eyubids in Egypt had to seek an alliance with the Kharzemians against the Crusaders, very much as Muslem Spain had sought Almoravid help in order to stop Christian invasion. But just as the Ata-Begs had taken advantage of the weakness of the Seljukids and supplanted them, so the Mamluks, the mercenaries of the Eyubids, managed to supplant their masters, towards the middle of the 13th century. Strangely enough, all these dynasties died of the same disease, one after another: the Pretorian Disease. Nevertheless, it was the Mamluks of Egypt who, after becoming Sultans, were to save both Islam and Europe from a Mongolian invasion.

THE MONGOLS. Until now, all the Turks who have invaded the Muslem world have been Muslems themselves, and often very fervently Orthodox; but they have come only from Central Asia. Their brothers of kindred race, the Mongols, inhabited more distant territories, and had ignored Islam. Pelliot says:

"The Mongols in the middle of the 13th century had for religion a loose form of Shamanism, and no fanaticism. The great Khan Guyuk himself was not hostile to Christians, having Christian members in his family. His two first successors had Christian mothers, and two of his principal ministers were Nestorian Christians.

The Mongols are often called Tartars, which was their primitive name. The name Mongol, which replaced it, was that of a small principality in Mongolia in the 12th century. They were called Mongols, both in Mongolia and in Central Asia, after the period of Genghiz-Khan. On the other hand, the name Tartar remained in use in the Western parts of the Mongol Empire, especially in the kingdom of the Golden Horde. Later, Europeans began to call all Turkish peoples Tartars, except the Ottomans. But as the name of a particular people, the word Tartar designates those Turks living on the Volga in Crimea, and in part of Siberia.

Genghiz-Khan, the founder of the Mongol Empire, was born of a noble family in the middle of the 12th century in the region which is now called Transbaikalia. His father had given him the name of Temutchin, and died when he was very young, so that he had to face want and privation for years. It can be said that he created his work out of nothing. As a matter of fact, he never left Mongolia, his native land, before he was fifty. There he had lived, leading a band of adventurers and living by hunting and razzias. It was during this period that he had the opportunity of helping the Chinese Kin Dynasty against the Nomadic princes who had been allowed to become powerful through lack of foresight. This brought him into public notice. Mongolia at that time was a prey to internal struggles, and he knew how to take advantage of them. Therefore, after some years of vicissitudes and trial Temutchin had imposed his authority upon the tribes living in half of the country by the year 1207. There is one important point to note here. Among Temutchin's companions of those early days were Muslem merchants who directed commercial enterprises between China and Mongolia. A few years later he used these same men as intermediaries between the Mongols and the Kharzemians. One can suppose that these same men first suggested to him the dominant idea of his reign: that is, the security of the great commercial route—the route of silk, as it was called in those days, the route between China and the West.

Three years later all Mongolia recognised Temutchin as master, and it is probable that it was then he took the name of Genghiz-Khan, the enigmatic title which the Chinese interpret as "Son of Heaven," though it may have been derived from the Mongol word "Tchink," which means strong. A Diet established the constitution of the Empire, and the rôle of one particular group in this assembly, the bodyguard, seems to have been most important. An iron discipline held the Mongol army together, and Yassa [1] (Law) was the principal cause of their triumph. The Yassa united the dispersed tribes into a single nation.

The first military expeditions of Genghiz-Khan were directed against China. Nevertheless, Genghiz-Khan turned East in 1209 and, taking advantage of the wars between the Kara-Khitais and Kharzemians, forced the Ouighur and Karluk princes of Central Asia to recognize his suzerainty. But Genghiz-Khan's wars in this direction really began in 1216. The Mongols, while in pursuit of enemy tribes, had in-

[1] Yassa means Law in old Turkish. Yassak in Turkey is used as "forbidden by the law." At the present time Yassa is still used as meaning "law" in Turkey.

vaded the Kirghiz steppes, where they encountered the troops of the Shah of Kharzem, and had to retire after an indecisive battle. But an event of economic importance became the cause of war in 1218. In response to an embassy sent by the Kharzem-Shah, Genghiz-Khan had sent out an important caravan, thus opening up commercial relations between the two peoples. This caravan consisting of Muslem merchants, was attacked, and the merchants massacred by the Kharzemians. Furthermore, the Kharzem-Shah refused reparation. It was then that Genghiz-Khan marched into Muslem territory at the head of an army composed of two hundred thousand men, inferior in numbers to the Kharzemian forces, it is true, but superior in organisation; and just as the Arab conquerors had once been received as deliverers, so were the Mongols received by the Muslems in Turkestan, who were being persecuted by a Turkish ruler who had passed from Nestorianism to Buddhism—for religious tolerance was assured them by the Mongols. The Kharzemian Empire had been enriched by the capture of Transoxiana from the Kara-Khitais, and Afghanistan from the Ghurids, and it dominated the principalities of Persia. Also, its might and grandeur humiliated the Caliph of Bagdad, who now reigned over a very small part of the country. Yet this Kharzem Empire was destroyed within a few months, and the Shah of the Kharzemians, tracked by Mongol cavalry, died of exhaustion. The two generals who were pursuing him continued their advance, subduing Northern Persia, crushing the Georgians in the Caucasus, and rallying around them the Turkish tribes who were settled in Europe. Meanwhile, Genghiz-Khan spread terror by his massacres during his conquest of the Bactrian country and of Afghanistan, and one of his sons ravaged Khorasan. All were swept aside before his onslaught. From Mongolia to Persia the unity of Asia was established, though partially on ruins. A new Alexander, though still half a savage, had traversed Asia. Before his death in 1227, Genghiz-Khan turned against the Chinese looters who pestered the caravans. While the Arabs, the Persians and the Muslem Turks had fought for an idea, the founder of the Mongol Empire, perhaps the greatest in extent which has ever existed, fought for the realisation of a terrestrial aim: the unification and security of Asia, and the suppression of religious wars. For this aim he sacrificed millions of lives. Nevertheless, one must admit that his impassibility and tenacity of purpose in most difficult circumstances lend an epic grandeur to this barbaric figure.

Genghiz-Khan designated Ogotai, his third son, as his successor, before he died. Nevertheless, according to the principle of nomadic monarchies which divide equally their tribes and appanages among the members of the reigning family, he divided his empire between his four sons. In accordance with the ancestral custom the youngest remained at home, and received the family heritage, which was that of Eastern Mongolia; and the eldest received the remotest part of the empire, which was that of the Golden Horde, a kingdom which extended from the Ukraine to the Sea of Aral. The second son reigned over two Turkestans, the Eastern and the Western. This was the land of the Turks, which had been in contact with Islam from the 8th century onwards.

Ogotai, who proved to be a mediocre emperor,

reigned over half of China, four-fifths of Russia, and Iran. In his time Chinese influence was supreme, owing to a great prime minister, but the other factions of the empire, that is, the Nestorians and the Muslems, struggled against this influence. Christians dreamed of an alliance between the Mongol Emperor and the Crusaders in order to crush Islam, a dream which was nearly realised at the time when Saint Louis sent crusading armies to Egypt. The Muslems, on the other hand, wanted the Mongol Emperor to restore the unity of Islam, and this aspiration was eventually realised by Timur, and later by the Ottoman Sultans. Both parties were in favour of Mongolic expansion, one persuading the Great Khan to conquer China, while the other led him to make an expedition into Persia, where a Muslem Turk, Djelal-ud-din, the last Kharzem, was in power and by his patronage had revived Persian nationalism. This Djelal-ud-din was a clumsy politician but a heroic and passionate figure who had previously taken refuge in India after a defeat. He took advantage of the Chinese expedition of the Mongols to return and continue his resistance, but began by fighting all his other neighbours, beginning with the Caliph in Bagdad and including Eyubis and the Seljukids of Anatolia. This reduced him to a state of complete isolation, so much so that he had to face the Mongols alone. When he died in 1231, everything went down before the Mongols, including Persia, Higher Mesopotamia, Georgia and the Seljukid Empire of Anatolia. The Mongols reached and forced their entrance into Europe. They submerged Russia, Poland, Hungary, and appeared before Vienna, naturally always taking advantage of the disunion among their enemies. Though European civilisation was saved by Ogotai's death, it had henceforward to reckon with the Mongols. Pope Innocent IV authorized the University of Paris to teach both Arabic and Tartar languages, and he also sent ambassadors to the Court of Karakurum where the Franciscan monk, Plan Carpin, saw the election of the Emperor Guyuk.

The Emperor Guyuk, who had been partial to the Nestorian and Armenian Churches as well as to Buddhism, died too soon to establish definitely the unity of the Empire. It was then that a Mongol princess, a Christian, and the niece of the last king of Karaites,[1] succeeded in placing a descendant of the youngest son of Genghiz-Khan on the throne in 1251. Mangu, or Meunke, was the first intellectual Mongol prince, and he established vocabularies, and admitted the Persian intelligentsia to his court, and, under the influence of his mother, showed a perfect religious tolerance, surrounding himself with Nestorians, Buddhists and Taoists, as well as with Muslems. He said to Cordelier Rubruquis: "All these religions are like the fingers of the same hand." This monk Rubruquis had been sent by Saint Louis, then at the head of a Crusade, with the proposition of an alliance against Islam. That was in 1254, but it was not the first suggestion of that sort. The king of Armenia had been clamouring for Mongol intervention against Islam. Meanwhile, Persia was in anarchy; the Assassins, whom the Seljukids had not been able to suppress completely, continued their gloomy exploits; and the Mamluks of Syria paralysed commerce. Hulagu, the brother of Mangu, a Buddhist prince, and

[1] Known as the priest Jean to the Mediaeval writers.

both the son and husband of Christian women, invaded Persia at the head of an army composed of Nestorian Turks from Central Asia. The Assassins and the Caliph were still preventing the unification of Asia under a Mongol hegemony. Hulagu attacked the Assassins, and after razing their fortresses to the ground, killed their chiefs in 1257. A year later he captured Bagdad, where though he spared the Christians, he ignominiously massacred the Caliph and his family. Traditional Islam had come to an end.

In the meantime, the second brother of Mangu, Kubilay, achieved the conquest of China; and by then the Emperor himself had died. The immense Mongol Empire was then divided into four great states: the Mongol Empire of China; the Khanat of Kiptchak (Russian Mongolia); the Khanat of Turkestan; and the Khanat of Persia. The centre of gravity of the empire was now transferred to the Far-East.

Meanwhile once more Persia seduced her conquerors, and the Mongols of Persia were converted to Islam and became men of cultivated taste. Even the new Emperor Kubilay, who had become nearly a Chinese, had several officials from Iran at his court in China. And it is at this period that Chinese as spoken by Chinese Muslems acquired Persian words. Persian had been for a long time the language of the official and elegant circles under the Turkish Dynasties of India and Central Asia, and the Seljukids had also adopted Persian as the official language. Hence Persian maintained its supremacy among the Turks until the Ottoman Turks replaced it by their own language.

The Christians of Armenia and Persia enjoyed

happy days under the Mongols, for Hulagu's policy was to favour the minorities and crush the last Muslem power in the East—namely the Mamluks of Egypt and Syria. In 1259, a Mongol army led by a Christian commander took Damascus and Aleppo. The Crusaders could then have joined them and finally subdued the Muslems; but alarmed by the increasing power of the Mongols, they hesitated, and thus gave time to the Sultan of Egypt to recuperate. A year later the Sultan of Egypt inflicted a defeat on the Mongol armies who had removed themselves too far from their base of operations, and were now forced to retreat to the other side of the Euphrates. This defeat was as decisive as that by the English at Poitiers: Mongol expansion had been definitely arrested. The direct result of this Muslem success was the Islamisation of the Mongol Khanat both in southern Russia and in Turkestan.

From this period onward, the Mongol Empire was stabilised, and travellers of all sorts, Italians, Arabs, Christian missionaries, and such famous figures as Marco Polo, Montcorvin and Pordenone could now move about in security and peace, while religions of diverse denominations freely multiplied their institutions. A peace, like the Roman Peace, now reigned in Asia.

The Resistance of Islam

Nevertheless centres of Islamic resistance still persisted.

On the one hand, the greatest of the Mamluk Sultans, Baibars, was not satisfied by merely driving out the Mongols. He reduced the power of the kings of Armenia, of the Crusaders, and of the Ismailians of

Syria. He had given refuge to the last of the Abassids, who had escaped the Mongols. He now very adroitly recognised him as Caliph, instituting himself the protector of the Caliphate, thus affirming his own legitimacy in the eyes of Orthodox Muslems.

On the other hand, the Seljukid Empire of Anatolia, another land of refuge for Sunnism, had been reduced to vassalage by the Mongols, who had divided it into small principalities. One of these became the cradle of the Ottoman Empire, owing to a Turkish clan which had taken flight from the Mongol invasion. These Ottomans were the veritable successors of the Seljukids; and like them, they became the champions of Orthodox Islam, and in the 16th century the Caliphate passed to the Ottoman Dynasty. In the 14th century the Ottomans quitted their territories on the Anatolian plateau, and by the help of their Janissaries, who were as severely disciplined as the Mongols, reached the Sea of Marmora, occupied the coasts from the Black Sea to the Gulf of Smyrna, crossed the Straits and began again the Mongol adventure in Europe.

Finally Islam established itself among the Mongols in Persia. The successor of Hulagu, like his father, was a Buddhist and the friend of Christians. He had married a daughter of the daughter of the Emperor Michael Paleologue, and had fought his cousin the Khan of Turkestan, thus beginning once more the wars of Iran against Turan as well as the struggle of Buddhism against Islam. Nevertheless, Islam gained ground and under the third prince of the Hulagu Dynasty was even the official religion for a short time; but his successor several times proposed a coalition against the Mamluks of Egypt to European monarchs, among them Philip the Magnificent. Nevertheless, Islam continued to gain ground in Persia, and forty years after the fall of the Caliphate of Bagdad it had triumphed completely. Of the Mongol princes only those of China escaped Islamisation; but with the conversion of the Persian Mongols, already degenerate and too refined by the effects of the civilisation of Persia, their kingdom fell into pieces. Local dynasties, Mongol or Persian, Sunnite or Shi'ite, emerged in different provinces, and with them internal wars.

Hence the political unity of Western Asia conceived by the Mongols was destroyed in the first years of the 14th century. However, this state of anarchy was brought to an end as usual by a strong man. Towards 1365, Timur-Leng, known as Tamarlane, a Turk and a Sunnite, the issue of a noble family of Transoxania, had begun to restore order in his country where the Mongol and the Turkish elements were continually fighting each other. Establishing his centre of operations in Samarkand, he decided to re-establish unity in Asia for the glory of Orthodox Islam. Though Persianised in culture, his three campaigns undertaken against the Persian Principalities, Afghanistan and Kharzem, were conducted with a ferocity worthy of the Mongols. After that Timur turned to Russia, where the Kiptchak Khanat was already disintegrating because of civil wars. India was the next perspective, a country which had hitherto remained on the margin of Mongol invasion. The Indo-Afghans were crushed in a battle from which Timur returned to Samarkand loaded with rich spoils. Finally, Timur turned to the Ottomans. Sultan Bayazid I had progressed in Asia

Minor, annexed Bulgaria, and destroyed at Nicopolis an army of Crusaders which had been sent against him. In 1396 he held the destiny of Europe in his hands. Six years after this date, Timur attacked Bayazid near Angora, and this famous battle changed the course of history by postponing the conquest of Constantinople by the Ottomans for half a century. Thus Timur became master in Asia. The princes of the West sent ambassadors to him who had saved them unwittingly. Only China, where the national Dynasty of Ming had overthrown the Mongols, held their own before Timur. He was preparing to conquer China, when he died at the beginning of the 15th century.

Once more the attempt to unify Asia had proved abortive. The Mamluks held their own both in Egypt and in Syria. In India, the Sultans of Delhi [1] were unable to prevent the rise of a series of local dynasties. In eastern Persia and Transoxania, a son and a grandson of Timur reigned at Herat and at Samarkand as great princes and patrons of the arts, following also the Mongol tradition of maintaining the security of the commercial routes, which, however, were destined to lose their importance because of the new vigour of Portuguese navigation. Western Persia and Mesopotamia, which had escaped from the Timurids, were scenes of internal conflict during the second half of the 15th century. The rivalries between the Turkoman clans, Ak-Koyunlu and Kara-Koyunlu,[2] are reminiscent of the struggles

1 Their ancestors had been originally in the service of the Ghurids, but had founded the first independent Dynasty of Ghazna.

2 Ak-Koyunlu means White Sheep, and Kara-Koyunlu Black Sheep.

of the Blacks and Whites in Italy, the Guelphs and the Gibelins; and just as Rome had, at an earlier date, sought the help of the Mongols against Islam, so now Venice sought the help of the Turkomans against the Turks of Anatolia.

Modern Times: Formation of Three Great Asiatic States

The Ottomans regained their strength after Timur's death. The conquest of Constantinople by Muhammed II in 1453 destroyed the Byzantine Empire, and the resistance of the Hungarian Hunyads, as well as that of the Albanian Skenderbeg, were in vain. The fall of the Byzantine capital which was as important as Bagdad, allowed the Turks to conquer the Balkans, annex the Islands of the Aegean, and get a foothold in Italy at Otranto. To the conquests of these two Peninsulas, that of the Balkans and half of Asia Minor, was added the conquest of Crimea: the Aegean Sea and the Black Sea became Ottoman.

The Ottoman Empire reached its zenith in the early days of the sixteenth century. Meanwhile Selim I turned his back on the West and marched eastward. In Persia, the Safevid Dynasty, by reorganising the country was becoming too powerful for Selim's peace of mind. These Safevids were descended from an ascetic who died in the Caspian, and who had the reputation of a saint. This ascetic had claimed descent from the seventh Ali-ite Imam; and therefore, was of Arab origin. His grandson declared himself a Shi'ite. The accession of the Safevids has much in common with that of the Abassids or the Fatimids. In the early days of the fifteenth century they created a religious order which spread its propaganda not only in Persia but in Asia Minor as well. They were the Sufis, who even after becoming rulers, remained the "Great Sufis" in the eyes of the Europeans. In 1490, Ismael, the conqueror of Persia, saw both his father and his brother fall in battle with the Turkomans. Though very young, experience and suffering matured him. He gathered around him a considerable number of partisans and with their help took advantage of the discord among the dozen princes who shared Persia, and defied them with success. In 1501 he proclaimed himself Shah of Persia, and established Shi'ism as the state religion. The birth of a rival empire to that of the Ottomans inaugurated the new century.

Shi'ism spread gradually in Asia Minor and massacres followed. War seemed inevitable between the Sunnite Ottomans and the Safevid Shi'ites. The bloody battle of Tchaldiran in 1514 was to have decided the destinies of the two powers. On that occasion the Turkish artillery routed the Persian cavalry, but Selim I did not take advantage of this victory, which could have been decisive. Deeming the Persians to have been sufficiently weakened, he went on to conquer Egypt; and just before his death he received the spiritual heritage of the Abassids who had been by now domesticated by the Mamluks. It seems, however, that Selim had taken the title of Caliph even before his conquest of Egypt, and that the supposed official abdication of the Abassids in his favour is nothing but a legend forged much later; but its consequences were far-reaching.

Meanwhile Persia survived her defeat at Tchaldiran, just as the Ottomans had survived theirs at the battle of Angora. The second of the Safevids ruled over a politically and religiously united Persia, and his reign lasted more than fifty years which, according to a chronicler was the longest reign after that of Mostansir the Fatimid. Religious and political wars with the Turks, who were at the height of their power, continued with the varying fortunes of battle. Busbeq, the Austrian ambassador to the Court of Soliman, the ally of the king of France and the greatest among the Sultans who laid siege to Vienna, writes: "Only Persia saves us from ruin. Her wars with Turkey give us respite."

The Ottoman Empire extended from the Danube to the cataracts of the Nile, and from the Euphrates to Gibraltar. In North Africa, the Turkish Corsairs had stopped the progress of the Spanish Christians by occupying the principal towns. Only Morocco was able to retain its independence thanks to the national and religious movements created by the Sherifs, movements which remind one of those of the Almoravids and the Almohads. These movements were provoked by the weakening of the Merinids, and were directed against the Christian invasions. Against these the Brotherhoods preached the Holy War, and the Holy War was led by the Saadian Sherifs who came from the Atlas, and claimed descent from the Ali-ite Imams, just as the Safevids of Persia had done. Bel says:

"The causes for the final triumph of Islam among the Berbers of Morocco from the 16th century onward are due to three facts: it had a mystical tendency and led its adherents to a purely mechanical ritual; the religious brotherhoods provided a concrete purpose for the apostles of mysticism; the cult of saints developed among the Berbers a religion which was in keeping with their native temperament and understanding, a religion for which Islam was a mere covering."

In the religious evolution of Islam, Turkey is only of secondary interest, and therefore it would not be useful to develop its history here. After Soliman's death in 1566, Turkey began to lose its power for offensive action. An inability to assimilate the conquered countries, the corruption of the administration, the caprices of various vezirs, harem intrigues, and the revolts of the Janissaries, so reminiscent of the risings of the pretorian guards of the Arab Caliphate, were among the principal causes which brought about its decline, and the Safevids knew how to profit by these weaknesses.

Shah-Abas, one of the great sovereigns of Persia, organised his army with the help of European instructors, and struggled against the Uzbegs, the Ottomans and the Portuguese. It was he who reconquered the sacred cities of Shi'ism, Nedjef and Kerbela. Further, he had given refuge to Armenians expelled from Turkey, and they in turn gave a magnificent impetus to Persia's commerce. During Abas's reign Persia entered definitely into economic and political relations with Europe, and in the first years of the 17th century she reached the zenith of her power. In the following century, attacked simultaneously by the Afghan and the Turkish Sunnites, she was saved by an adventurer of genius, Nadir Shah, who proposed to include Shi'ism among the Orthodox Madhabs [1] and afterwards restored Sun-

[1] See page 121.

nism in Persia, contemplating even the establishment of a new religion. We will see later how, in the 19th century, a new religious doctrine derived from Islam arose in Persia under the name of Babism.

Finally, a third Empire came into existence in Western Asia. While Ismael was consolidating the basis of Safevid power in Persia, Baber, a descendant of Timur on his father's side, and a descendant of Genghiz-Khan on his mother's side, began to work for the religious and political unification of India. Baber had inherited the principality of Ferghana from his father, but he had not been able to maintain himself in Central Asia. Crossing the Hindu-Kush, he prepared for the conquest of India. This was a repetition of Ghaznevid and Ghurid history and, like them, Baber descended into India through Afghanistan. Baber's admirable Memoirs which may be compared with those of Caesar, tell us of his life and his heroic struggles. This great man was not yet fifty when he died in 1530. For a century after his death, the Empire of the Great Mongols which he had founded persisted with an incomparable splendour. In the following century, the rivalries of the Afghans, Mahrattas, French and English succeeded in allowing the Mongol Empire only a nominal existence under the British tutelage. In 1856, that is, six centuries less a year after the fall of the Abassid Caliphate, the last prince of the Mongol Dynasty in India finished his days in exile.

We see now the predominant parts the Turanians of the East, that is, the Mongols, and the Turanians of the West, that is, the Turks, have played in the history of Asia. During their first period the Mongols tried to establish a political and economic unity in Asia under a Laic State, which logically had to suppress the Caliphate. During their second period the Mongols turned towards the Far-East, and the Turks took their stand in the Orient, and became the supporters of Orthodox Islam. Between the two, Persia, in spite of the mixture of races among her peoples proved the permanence of the Indo-European genius.

In brief, it was these three great states which definitely established Islam in Asia; though one must not forget the pacific penetration of Islam into various other countries. We know already how[1] Islam gained a foothold in Madagascar, in the Malay archipelago and in China through the medium of merchants and travellers. After reaching Sumatra and the Moluccas, Islam established itself in Java from the 16th century onward, and from there gained Borneo, and then in the following century established itself in Celebes. In China, in spite of there being only six million Muslems, the influence of Islam increased, the reason being that the Muslems were grouped at important centres, such as Turkestan, which had always played a decisive part in China's destiny. Islam was introduced into Indo-China in the eleventh century by the Arab navigators, and from there was propagated into the land of Tchams in the 14th and 15th centuries, and into Cambodia in the 16th. The Islamisation of Africa continued slowly. In Ethiopia it began in the 12th century, and its progress was never interrupted. In the Sudan, we have seen how the Berbers imposed Islam on the Western regions where several small kingdoms had

[1] See page 69.

risen on the ruins of the Ghana Empire. Another century had to pass before a new empire, that of the Mandingue, was to establish its hegemony. In the 16th century, owing to the conquest of the country by the Pagan Peuls, Islamic progress was retarded for a time, but began to accelerate once more in the 18th century. Into central Sudan Islam had begun to penetrate from the 15th century onwards, but in Eastern Sudan only the Nubians had accepted it until the 16th century, after which there also it began to gain more adherents. Finally, we know that in Arabia itself certain tribes, such as the Ahl Morra, who were not yet Islamised, have been recently converted.

The Last Religious Innovations

AKBAR. The third member of Baber's Dynasty, Akbar, the great emperor who reigned during the first half of the 16th century, was a man of genius. His strategic and administrative abilities were only equalled by the grandeur of his philosophic and religious conceptions. Like Marcus Aurelius, Akbar was a sage on a throne. His dominant trait seems to have been his enlightened tolerance. Though born and bred in Sunnite traditions, he preferred Shi'ite doctrine as being more favourable to religious enthusiasm, and this led him to substitute Persian for Arabic in his states. From Shi'ism he passed naturally into a most advanced stage of Mysticism, and himself became a perfect Sufi. Under the influence of this exalted Mysticism he permitted the use of wine and the eating of pork, denied the eternity of hell-fire, declaring that the damned could be saved through a series of reincarnations, a belief which he had borrowed from Brahmanism.[1] Further, in 1593, he authorised Hindus who had been Islamised by force to return to their original religion. Whether by personal conviction or politics, Akbar finally reached a conception of Deism which considered divergencies of doctrine or ritual as secondary. His sympathies were at the same time for Brahmanism, Buddhism and Christianity, whose priests he assembled in his presence for discussions of their religions. In brief, he dreamed of a religious syncretism and arrived at a deism that should be without formal clergy. The visible symbols of the ancient Persian religion which the Mazdeens had revealed to him. In practice, this deism of Akbar's had few followers, nevertheless it proved a blow to Orthodox Islam in India. His son and successor hastily returned to Orthodoxy; but the Orthodox reaction against Akbar which had dangerous repercussions was to take place a century later under Aurengzeb.[2] Nevertheless, Akbar's syncretism was one of the most vigorous breaks with traditional Islam.

Syncretism has always found a favourable reception in India. Goldziher says: "India, with its variegated religious phenomena, appears to the student as a school of comparative religions; and in reality it is so." This mixture of contradictory beliefs appeared once more in a doctrine in the Punjab under the name of Ahmidiya. The adherents of this doctrine carried on an active propaganda in English, both in Europe and in Asia. The leader of the sect

1 The Sikh sect in India with whom Akbar was on friendly terms admitted metempsychosis. See Encyclopedia of Islam, article Sikhs.

2 The mystical tendencies and conciliatory conceptions of Dara Shikuh, Aurengzeb's elder brother, were influenced by Akbar's ideas.

was Ghulam Ahmed, who died in 1908; and he had already made an exposition of his principles in a work published in 1880. The death of Jesus Christ remains obscure in the Koran. While one passage in the Koran denies the crucifixion,[1] another passage [2] affirms it. Ghulam Ahmed made use of the lack of precision on this issue by declaring that the death of Jesus was only apparent, and that he escaped from his tomb to preach the true religion in India, where he had eventually died. His sepulchre was definitely at Srinagar, according to the Ahmidiya sect. A Sunnite Fatwa naturally condemned this invention. But on the other hand the same syncretic tendency appears in the idea of Mahdism peculiar to the Ahmidiya sect. While the Orthodox considered the Messiah and the Mahdi as two different persons, Ghulam Ahmed the founder of the Ahmidiya sect conceived them as united in one person, and declared himself to be the incarnation. According to him also, the mission of the Mahdi was to be strictly of a pacific nature and the Jihad was understood to be not a war, but a form of intellectual propaganda. Ahmed aimed at uniting Muslems, Hindus and Christians in one faith.

WAHHABISM. The idea which gave rise to Wahhabism in the 18th century was diametrically opposed to that of Akbar. The Wahhabite movement wanted to return to the primitive orthodoxy of Islam in Arabia. We have already noted that Wahhabism

[1] "And their saying: surely we have killed the Messiah, Jesus, the son of Mary, the apostle of Allah; and they did not kill him, nor did they crucify him" (Chap. 4:157).

[2] "When Allah said: O Jesus! I will cause you to die and exalt you in My presence, and clear you of those who disbelieve. . . ." (Chap. 3:54).

was based on a more exaggerated form of Almohad monotheism.[1] As a matter of fact, their doctrine rested strictly on the text of the Koran, with the Sunna, and rejected all interpretation and commentary. Wahhabism found elements of polytheism in Orthodox Islam into which the cult of prophets, of saints and tombs had crept. For them, neither the prophets nor the saints had by definition the knowledge of the hidden truth without Allah's revelation. To consider the prophets and the saints as intercessors was like superimposing a power over that of Allah. It was to be only on the Day of Judgment that Muhammed was to obtain the power of intercession from Allah. Hence Wahhabism could not accept the honouring of any created object such as tombs, even of prophets, by acts of prostration, by circumambulations, or by kissing the stones as sacred objects. Wahhabism also rejected superstitions, such as a belief in auspicious or evil days, in precursory signs and in soothsayers; and they forbade the taking of an oath in the name of the Prophet or in the name of any member of his family. They also banished alcoholic drinks, smoking, music, dancing and gambling, like the Kharidjite Abadhites.[2]

Wahhabism derives its name from its founder, Ibn Abd-al-Wahab, who died in 1787. Wahhabite doctrines did not spring from Kharidjism, as might be supposed; but from the Hanbalite Rite which, at least theoretically advocated a return to primitive Sunna.[3] Hanbalism had been revived in the early days of the 14th century by a remarkable theologian,

1 See page 221.
2 See page 177.
3 See page 120.

Ibn-Taimiya, who had died in prison. In the 18th century, Ibn-Abd-al-Wahab, under the influence of Tamiya's doctrine, founded Wahhabism, which was essentially a violent reaction against the cult of saints. Towards 1740, Ibn-Abd-al-Wahab and Ibn Saud united for the purpose of propagating Wahhabism, the former representing the spiritual, and the latter the temporal aspect. They founded a state in Nedjd which disquieted the Sublime Porte. In 1802 they pillaged the Shi'ite sanctuaries, and in 1806 followed the example of the Karmathians [1] by occupying Mecca, and destroying mosques and pulpits. They respected only the Kaaba, and they captured Medina and violated the Prophet's tomb. Their raids naturally suspended pilgrimages to Mecca; and meanwhile their movement spread into Syria and Mesopotamia. It was then that, in 1811, Muhammed-Ali, who had beaten the Mamluks,[2] received an order from the Sublime Porte to suppress the Wahhabites. He did not succeed until 1818, and then his success was in vain for the Wahhabite state reconstituted itself soon afterwards. About the same time an Indian, Ahmad of Bareilly, was propagating analogous doctrines in his country, where pagan survivals and the cult of saints were prevalent among Muslems through the polytheistic influence of Brahmanism. To-day Wahhabism dominates the major part of Arabia both politically and religiously; and its sphere of influence extends even beyond Arabia into the neighbouring countries, such as Mesopotamia and Somali, particularly since Ibn Saud overthrew the ephemeral Sherifian Dynasty in Hedjaz, in 1924.

[1] See page 160.

[2] The adversaries of Napoleon.

BABISM AND BAHAISM. While Wahhabism, a strictly Arab movement, proposed to lead back to its primitive sources, Babism and its offspring Behaism, an exclusively Persian movement, tried to enlarge Islam. Wahhabism is confined to Arabia, but Bahaism has spread throughout Asia and passed on to America with astonishing rapidity. As a matter of fact, Bahaism is not so much a new sect as a new religion, though it is derived from Islam. The Persian Government understood this from the very day Babism made its appearance, and tried to destroy it by every available means. In its early days Babism was not without some analogy to the Lutheran movement, in that it was a puritanical revolt against the official clergy. On the other hand, the members of the Persian official clergy, the Mullahs, tried to represent the Babis as anarchists.

We know that the conception of the Mahdi, that is, the return of the hidden Imam, occupies an important place in Shi'ism.[1] The founder of Babism, Mirza Ali Muhammed, took that idea as his starting point. Mirza-Ali Muhammed was born in Shiraz in 1819, and during a pilgrimage to Kerbela, the Shi'ite Sanctuary, he had met a member of the Shaikhis sect of Shi'ism. The doctrine of the Shaikhis sect was an intense cult of the hidden Imam, and was strongly in opposition to the doctrine of the Akhbaris, the partisans of tradition.[2] Mirza Ali Muhammed returned to Shiraz very much under the influence of the Shaikhis, and began to preach against the official clergy. The Shaikhis doctrine led Mirza Ali Muhammed to declare himself Bab while under the

[1] See page 186.
[2] See page 188.

influence of a nocturnal ecstasy[1] in 1844. The title Bab was not a new one, but had been given by Ismailians, Druzes and Nusairis to some of their dignitaries. Further, Bab, in addition to his preaching, produced a book composed of an allegorical interpretation of the Koran, a work which reminds one of that of Ismailism.[2] It rallied to its doctrines all those who, tired of the rigorism of Orthodoxy, dreamed of liberty and equality, and waited for the Mahdi. The movement gained such force that Bab was imprisoned, but before his arrest he had succeeded in converting one of the leading clergy of Teheran to his doctrine, a man who had come to Shiraz for the purpose of opposing Bab's teachings. Bab's partisans carried on with his teaching while he was in prison. Among them was a woman called Zerrina Taj (Chrysostephane), surnamed Qurrat-ul-ain, meaning the Solace of the Eye. She was both beautiful and intelligent, and was at the same time a pioneer of Feminism in Persia. Her activities led the Persian government to a more rigorous persecution of the Babis. Babism had its first martyrs, and the story of the heroic resistance of the Babis in their fortresses at Mazendran is told by Gobineau. Hence Babism, from being a purely religious movement became political. In order to arrest the movement which was gaining adherents all the time, the Persian government decided to strike at the head of it. Bab was condemned to death and shot; but the Government had to use Christian soldiers to execute him. The first round of shot severed the cords with which

1 Bab means the Door, the door which opens the knowledge of divine truth.

2 The date corresponds to the thousandth year of the mysterious disappearance of the 12th Imam.

he had been suspended. If he had had the presence of mind to take refuge among the crowd of spectators he would have been saved; but dazed and exhausted, he ran towards the soldiers, who hacked him to death with their swords. That was in 1850.

His death did not discourage the Babis. On the contrary, they continued their propaganda with greater zeal. In 1852, three of them attacked the Shah and wounded him. The repressive measures taken against them were terrible, the details of which are given by Gobineau and Nicolas. Among the martyrs, was the unfortunate Qurrat-ul-ain who was first strangled, after which her corpse was burnt on the pyre.

What were the dangerous innovations which Bab proposed? His doctrine implied a religious and social revolution. For the Koran of Muhammed he substituted his own Koran, which he claimed to have had revealed. While the traditional Koran attaches great importance to legal purity, Bab considered everything to be essentially pure, and that purity in practice depended on temperance. Of Bab's social reforms the most important were the abolition of the old divorce laws, and a considerable increase in the dignity and liberty of women—a liberty which has become a fact in the Orient to-day. In general, Bab maintained that one must live, not according to the letter, but according to the spirit of the religious law—an attitude which reminds one of that of Christians in their early reactions against Judaism. But to these admirably reasonable ideas Bab added arithmetical combinations analogous to those of the Ismailians and the Hurufis. God had created the world out of seven attributes; and the number 19 must be considered sacred because it has the numerical value of the letters which compose the word "Wahid," meaning the Only God.

After Bab's death one of his disciples became head of the sect. This was Mirza Yahya, surnamed "Subh-e-Ezel," meaning the Dawn of Eternity. He had taken refuge in Bagdad, but the Turkish Government first ordered him to Constantinople and then to Adrianople. In 1863, while he was in Adrianople, a schism divided Babism. Mirza-Yahya's half-brother Mirza Husain, surnamed Baha-Ullah, meaning Divine Splendour, declared himself to be the person announced by Bab in the manner of the Ismailians.

Subh-e-Ezel died in 1912, and his followers, called the Azalis, remained faithful to the Babi doctrine; but they have since gradually disappeared. Baha-Ullah's party, known as the Bahais, continued its active propaganda both in Persia and outside. What are the differences between these sects?

Babism, in comparison with Shi'ism, represents a progress towards religious liberalism, but remains Islamic in general and Persian in particular. Baha-Ullah, on the other hand, meant to establish a cosmopolitan and universal religion, and with this aim was a desire for a universal language. He did not propose to abolish the previous religions, but to unite them around one and the same idea. For him all religions were good, and what was necessary for unity among them was the abolition of their dogmas and rituals. The prophets, he said, did not cancel each other, but all proclaimed the same principles, and were in a way intermediary between the Supreme Spirit and men. The Supreme Spirit can be known by its attributes. In his view the one thing needful was to love God, for love was the condition of progress, and the basis of universal law.

In practice, Bahaism has no special rites; for, according to Bahaism, religion must manifest itself in actions and not in ceremonies. Hence, there was no sacerdotal hierarchy. Socially all human beings, both men and women, have the same rights. War must be abolished, and all differences settled by arbitration.

Briefly, Bahaism was more of a moral code than a religion, though a moral code with a mystical tendency. Abas Effendi, however, the son and successor of Baha-Ullah, was greatly inspired by the rationalism of the West, and this had a further influence on the sect.

MODERNISM. Modern ideas have influenced Islam, particularly since the French Revolution, and generally through the intermediary of France.

It is not necessary to dwell on the political aspects of these modernist tendencies which were helped by the development of the press. In one way or another they have usually taken the form of nationalism; and since the abolition of the Ottoman Caliphate by the Angora Assembly and the fall in 1924 of the Great Sherif of Mecca who had proclaimed himself Caliph, these nationalist movements have been based on some realization of historical forces. The question of the Caliphate seems to have lost its metaphysical importance.

From the religious point of view the Modernists want to re-establish Idjtihad, that is the right to free discussion and deliberation.[1]

In India, Sir Saiyyid Ahmad, who died in 1898,

[1] See page 122.

and founded the Aligarh University, had written a Neo-Mutazelite commentary of the Koran, which is definitely a rationalist interpretation. His followers believe in the necessity of resolutely adapting Islam to the needs of the modern world.

In Egypt, Muhammed Abdu, who died in 1905, and was a disciple of Djemal-ud-Din-Afghani, who died in 1897, rejected European influences and returned to the teachings of the Koran and the Sunna. But he interpreted the Koranic text in a way which includes concepts which are equivalent to those of modern science. For example, the Djinns[1] of the Koran are taken to be microbes. Such interpretations he used to prove the power of divination of Islam, and its superiority over other religions. Abdu proposed an adaptation of Western science in Islamic terms, an attempt which reminds one of Ashari and Ghazali.

In Turkey, the Swiss Code has replaced the traditional Muslem Law; the religious Brotherhoods are suppressed; and the Latin alphabet has been adopted in place of the Arabic alphabet, which had been used by Turks for centuries.

Everywhere in the East, the emancipation of women is gaining ground; and European thinkers are read and discussed, and are exercising considerable influence.

A wind of rationalism seems to blow from every side among Muslem intellectuals; but who can affirm that the call of mysticism will not again be heard some day in the Islamic world in accordance with the eternal law of action and reaction?

[1] See page 131.

Index